A TALE OF TWO ROADS

An Early History
of Hull F.C. and Hull K.R.

by

Michael E. Ulyatt

With Research Assistance
from Peter Ablitt

HUTTON PRESS
1996

Published by

The Hutton Press Ltd.,
130 Canada Drive, Cherry Burton,
Beverley, East Yorkshire HU17 7SB

Printed and bound by
Clifford Ward & Co. (Bridlington) Ltd.,
55 West Street, Bridlington, East Yorkshire, YO15 3DZ

ISBN 1 872167 78 0

CONTENTS

ACKNOWLEDGEMENTS

In a time of great uncertainty for rugby league's future, I have been overwhelmed with the support given to me in compiling this book. I am especially grateful to Max Gold for putting his comprehensive collection of rugby league memorabilia at my disposal; to research assistant Peter Ablitt for his invaluable contribution made to the research for and producing much of the text for this publication. Peter's contribution was in part sponsored by a Community Action volunteer placement at Hull College's Local History Unit, and the work was completed during a Skills Advantage adult training placement in the Local History Unit. The author gratefully acknowledges the part played by the Local History Unit at Hull College and unit supervisor Chris Ketchell in supporting this research project; to Bill Dalton and Chris Elton for statistical help; to Andy Gray for copies of fixture lists; and finally to Charles and Dae Brook of Hutton Press for having the courage to publish this, my fourth book on local rugby league history.

Mike Ulyatt
September 1995

Hull F.C. Season 1881-1882
Back Row: L. Whitehead, H. L. Smith, G. W. Braithwaite, D. R. Lovell, F. Winter,
J. Wilson, F. Jones, A. H. Tyacke, E. Robinson.
Middle Row: W. Close, G. A. Hoskins (Capt.), W. F. B. Calvert.
In Front: L. A. Smith, A. Smithson, J. F. B. Calvert, E. M. Braithwaite.

Chapter One
MEMORIES

Tom pulled up his coat collar as a bit of protection against the bitter north easterly wind. He looked down on the Boulevard pitch from the top of the terracing at the Airlie Street end. The score board man was taking the numbers down and the ground was rapidly emptying. His favourites Hull F.C. had just beaten the mighty Wigan. A Friday night in mid-January was not the ideal time for watching rugby league but Tom, along with some five thousand other fans, had been warmed through by the Black and White's emphatic victory.

"Well done — you deserved to win" said the man in the red and white scarf as he passed by.

"Aye" said Tom "It's a welcome change. You've hammered us a lot over the years. Safe journey home."

Tom's mind went back to the first match he had seen at the Boulevard, some forty years ago. Was it Hull 'A' against Hunslet 'A'? He had caught the 'Fish Dock' bus on Sculcoates Lane at 2 o'clock on a Saturday afternoon together with his two pals, Colin and Cyril. The blue and white single decker bus was packed with fans — men, women and boys. Almost all of them were wearing black and white scarves. Cigarette smoke filled the air together with the smell of fish left by the bobbers from the Fish Dock who had just got off the bus after leaving work. There was a continuous buzz of conversation as the bus conductor collected the fares. "Is Charlie Booth playing today?"; "Who's the ref? — Oh no, not bloody Davies. We've had it then." Tom remembered it all so clearly as if it were only yesterday. Getting off the bus at the top of Albert Avenue and walking along Anlaby Road, waiting for a train to pass at the railway crossing at the top of Selby Street. Half walking, half running down the Boulevard, soaking up the atmosphere, expectant. Reaching the ground, paying the admission money at the turnstile and buying a programme. What an adventure it had all seemed to be. The three of them climbed up to the top of the shale embankment. To their right, the Threepenny Stand was packed full. Everyone booed when Hunslet ran out and cheered when their favourites appeared.

Tom sighed. "How many times have I been to this ground since then." Memories of past matches and great players came flooding back. The local derby matches against Rovers on Good Friday and Christmas Day morning when a character named Shep and his entourage would walk around the ground, pushing a pram bedecked in black and white and carrying a small coffin with a red robin on top to the strains of 'Old Faithful' and 'Who Killed Cock Robin?'; Bruce Ryan racing down the wing; Ginger Burnell diving over for a try in the corner; Freddie Miller kicking virtually the full length of the field; referee 'Sergeant Major' Eric Clay enjoying the crowd's banter, especially from the Threepenny Stand; What memories. What characters. Roy Francis,

Tommy Glynn, The Drake twins, Tommy Harris, Harry Markham, Bob Coverdale, Colin Hutton, Arthur Keegan, Keith Boxall, Alf Macklin, Clive Sullivan, Keith Tindall, Lee Crooks, Gary Kemble, Peter Sterling, Charlie Stone, Steve "Knocker" Norton. Face upon face flashed through Tom's mind. His eyes filled with tears as he slowly walked out of the ground. Discarded drink cans rattled across the concrete. Tom gazed up at the hospitality boxes where he could see soberly suited businessmen and women enjoying themselves. How many matches had they ever seen he thought. Did they even understand the game? He hurried through the crowded car park, edging his way past the players' sponsored cars and carefully stepping over the thick cables stretching out from the two large television vehicles. Tom remembered Johnny Whiteley telling him how he had walked from his home along Hessle Road and down the Boulevard and Airlie Street to play his first match against Hull K.R., mingling with the fans and quietly chuckling at the good-natured banter directed at him. Tom didn't begrudge present day players anything. They were complete athletes, playing in the hardest sport in the world. Most with a genuine love of their game. But he couldn't help remembering how his heroes seemed to have their feet on the ground. Most players then had a full time job and somehow seemed closer to the fans. More approachable perhaps?

Tom reached his own car and gazed back over his shoulder. The voice startled him. "Good game, eh Dad?" He'd been so engrossed in his own thoughts he'd forgotten his son had been with him.

Tom had taken him to rugby from an early age, including three trips to Wembley, two to Old Trafford and visits to Headingley, Boothferry Park and Elland Road. He seemed to have inherited his Dad's enthusiasm for the game. "We'll have to watch all our rugby on the telly in the pub next season, eh Dad?" Tom smiled. "You can son. I'll be watching cricket. Summer rugby won't be for me. I can see me watching Beverley and West Hull in the winter. What else would I do on a Saturday afternoon?" In his mind Tom knew the game had to change. Perhaps its new image would draw support from the young but he would always have his memories. He wondered what Colin and Cyril would make of it all.

It happened right under referee Wingfield's nose. There seemed to be no reason for it. Rovers were already beating Huddersfield 5—0 in a league match when John Taylor was seen to throw a punch at Anderson as he tackled him, seven minutes into the second half. There was no doubt about it, Taylor had to go, thousands of fans had seen the incident. Sam was stood behind the posts at the Holderness Road end of Craven Park, in front of the towering Tote Information Board that Friday night. Someone behind him muttered "That's Taylor out of our Wembly team." Rovers had beaten Oldham 12—2 in the cup semi-final after a 5—5 draw and an abandoned replay to reach the Wembley cup final against Widnes in just a few days time. The result of the sending off was that Taylor was suspended for one match, therefore missing the 1964 final and the highlight of every player's career, an appearance at Wembley. Sympathy went out to the player and the Craven Park episode had remained in

Sam's memory together with the stories his grandfather told him of the days when the Robins were real chopping blocks. Despite the regular defeats, his grandfather was a loyal fan. He had worked for Hull Corporation Transport, firstly as a tram driver and latterly driving petrol buses along Holderness Road. The 'bus shed' was situated right next to Craven Park and most drivers and their conductors would hurry to finish their shift and park their buses overlooking the pitch where they would all sit on the top deck of the buses and watch the match for free! Games were played on a Saturday afternoon then.

Sam chuckled to himself at the memories. "We've always seemed to be the poor relations in Hull" Sam mused. Years of struggle, glorious success when it came. Could it have been any different? Despite the large population of the East Hull housing estates — Bilton Grange, Longhill, Greatfield and now Bransholme — the Robins had always struggled to attract big crowds. But Sam was sure of one thing — once a red and white fan, always a red and white fan. It was his game.

'A fast forward game'.
*An engraving from Athletics and Football, The Badminton Library of Sports and
Pastimes by Montague Shearman and published by Longmans, Green and Co.
of London in 1889.*

'A loose scrimmage'.
*An engraving from Athletics and Football, The Badminton Library of Sports and
Pastimes by Montague Shearman and published by Longmans, Green and Co.
of London in 1889.*

Chapter Two
IN THE BEGINNING

Rugby was introduced into Hull direct from the public schools by several old scholars of Cheltenham, Rugby, Marlborough and St. Peter's — particularly the Hutchinsons, B. Lambert, E. Waltham, R. J. Wade and the five Scott brothers, F. A. Scott, G. Cooper Scott, Henry Scott, Charles Scott and J. Scott. Their father was the Rev. John Scott, vicar of St. Mary's, Lowgate and he also helped to run a rifle volunteer group.

Meetings were held and the Hull Football Club was formed in 1865. The club's first ground was at Woodgates Hall in North Ferriby, the home of the Harrisons and although some difficulty was experienced in finding suitable opponents, games were arranged with Bramham College, Newark, Louth and St. Peter's York.

Later they were playing Bradford, York, Leeds and Huddersfield but because of the distances which had to be travelled to Hull by steam train, the club's President, John Loft, rented a "ground" at Selby opposite the Londesborough Arms. This was roughly halfway between Hull and the "far" West Riding and the landlord did not charge a rent for the field, allowing his pub to be used as changing rooms for both teams and he probably gained from the sale of beer and food after the matches. This arrangement did not last long and a third ground was found, the Rifle Barracks at Londesborough Street in Hull.

Saturday, 2nd February 1867.
The Hull and North Lincolnshire Times,

FOOTBALL MATCH — On Saturday a football match was on the Rifle Corps ground, between the Hull and Lincoln clubs. After a severe contest, the victory resulted in favour of the Hull side, who obtained two goals, although one of the goals was obtained by the Lincoln side kicking the ball through their own goal, which of course the Hull players claimed. The first goal was kicked by Mr. Hutchinson. The sides were:- Hull: E. Waltham (capt.), J. F. Waltham, H. E. Cator, R. J. Wade, B. Lambert, Hutchinson, F. Galloway, J. McCormick, H. Ayre, A. Ayre, A. Spratt. Lincoln: D. J. Grantham (capt.), W. Lowe, M. Lipthorpe, H. Allott, Melville, T. Bainbridge, E. Parham, J. Carlin, W. Oliver, W. Dawher, A. Marshall. After the match both clubs partook of an excellent dinner, at Bainton's Victoria Hotel.

Saturday, 7th December 1867.
The Hull and North Lincolnshire Times,

FOOTBALL — THE HULL CLUB v BRAMHAM COLLEGE. — This match was played on Saturday last, on the ground of the latter, and resulted in an easy victory for Bramham which secured six goals in the short space of two hours. The game was played according to the association rules. Hull won the toss, and chose to kick in the direction of the house goal. Play commenced at 12.45 pm. Bramham soon ran the ball up to their opponents' goal, and, after a struggle of about half an hour duration, kicked their first goal. After each kick-off, the ball was rapidly taken down to the Hull goal, whose defenders laboured in vain against the superior numbers of their opponents, who had 15 to their 12. The superior activity of Bramham made the weight of their adversaries of no avail. T. E. Plint and G. Hill were excellent backs: and C. H. Potts, R. L. Plint and W. Wager, as half-backs, successfully resisted almost every attempt to carry the ball through them. The rest, as ups, displayed considerable activity. The following is a list of the players:- Hull: E. Waltham (capt.) R. J. Wade, A. Spratt, F. Brodrick, F. H. Galloway, H. Saxelbye, E. Bromley, R. E. Turnbull, E. A. Wade, F. S. Kelsey, W. Eldridge, G. Jackson. Bramham: T. E. Plint (capt.) R. L. Plint, R. C. Richards, G. A. Hill, A. Ballance, H. Waind, W. S. Laing, J. Burnyeat, C. H. Potts, A. A. Mellor, G. L. Batley, A. L. Knight, W. Sager, A. Turner, G. A. Milligan. This is the second match the Bramham Club has played this season: the former one with Leeds Grammar School, which terminated in an easy victory for Bramham, who secured three goals to their opponents' none.

Saturday, 7th March 1868.
The Hull and North Lincolnshire Times,

FOOTBALL — BRAMHAM COLLEGE v HULL — RETURN MATCH
This match was played on the ground at Bramham on Saturday last. The toss being won by the Hull captain, the ball was kicked off by the opposite side, who kicked for the "ash tree" goal. For the first half hour the game was very evenly contested, but the next quarter showed the weak points in the Hull team who, although superior to their opponents in weight, had not the same amount of wind. About this time the first goal was kicked for Bramham by Batley. Two more were eventually kicked for Bramham by Messrs. A. Mellor and Laing. Thus, the return match, like the former, resulted in favour of the Bramham team. Where all on both sides played so well, it would be difffficult to draw a distinction, if we except the extraordinary long kicking of the Hull captain. The players were:- for Bramham College: Messrs. T. Plint, captain: G. Hill, J. Barnyeat, W. Sager, Waud, A. Mellor, Laing, Batley, R. Plint, Knight, C. Schofield, Hull: Messrs: Waltham, captain: R. Wade, E. Wade, Lambert, F. Scott, Saxelby, Spratt, McLaren, Armytage, Ayre, A. Ormorod. The last named played as a substitute for Mr. Turnbull.

Saturday, 6th November 1869.
The Hull and North Lincolnshire Times,

HULL FOOTBALL CLUB — An opening match was played on Saturday afternoon between the members of the club whose initials were included from A to M, and the remainder. The "First Half" were palpably overmatched, and a goal was soon obtained for the "Second Half" by Mr. R. J. Wade, and after a short struggle, Mr. Waltham kicked another. Sides were then selected by Mr. Lambert and Mr. R. J. Wade, and a capital game was played, which resulted in favour of the latter side by three goals, obtained by Mr. F. A. Scott (2) and Mr.

R. J. Wade (1), against two goals scored by Mr. F. K. Gibson and Mr. C. Thompson. The season was commenced most auspiciously, and it is to be regretted that the number of spectators was not large. Play will commence throughout the season at 2.30 pm, every Saturday.

Saturday, 20th November 1869.
The Hull and North Lincolnshire Times,

FOOTBALL — HULL CLUB v ST. PETER'S SCHOOL, YORK. — This match was played at York on Saturday, in very unfavourable weather, and resulted in a victory for Hull by two goals. The school having won the toss played with the wind, and for nearly an hour neither side obtained any decisive advantage. St. Peter's secured a touchdown, but failed in the punt out; at length a splendid kick by R. Waltham obtained a goal, and another was soon kicked by R. J. Wade. Although several gallant charges were made by the boys, they could not retrieve their defeat, the weight of the club telling very much. Hull only played nine men, the weather preventing two from appearing. St. Peter's commenced with eleven, but one was hurt early, and had to retire. Both teams played well, especially the brothers Waltham for Hull, and Robertson for York; and the goal keeping of Spratt for Hull was much admired. The Hull team consisted of E. Waltham (captain), R. Waltham, R. J. Wade, E. A. Wade, A. Spratt, F. A. Scott, C. Thompson, and H. Saxelby. Our correspondent was unable to secure the York list.

Saturday, 29th January 1870.
The Hull and North Lincolnshire Times,

HULL FOOTBALL CLUB — On Saturday a match was played at Selby between Hull and Selby football clubs. The Hull club was powerfully represented, and won easily by two goals to none. The goals were kicked by Messrs. E. Waltham and F. Moss.

Saturday, 12th February 1870.
The Hull and North Lincolnshire Times,

HULL FOOTBALL CLUB — On Saturday last this club played the Louth Club at the Rifle Barracks, and gained another easy victory. The weather was very bad, and the ground in wretched order, but the Hull club secured four goals, Louth not scoring one. The goals were obtained by (1) Mr. E. Waltham, (2) Mr. Lambert, and (3 & 4) Mr. Hutchinson. The club has been very fortunate this season, having won four matches without the loss of a goal.

A meeting held in the George Hotel, Hull on 10th October 1870 decided 'it was not lawful to take up the ball when it was rolling and no player should stand on the goal bar to interrupt its going over.'

Saturday, 15th October 1870.
The Hull and North Lincolnshire Times,

HULL FOOTBALL CLUB — The annual meeting of the members of this club was held at the George Hotel on Monday last. There was a numerous attendance. It was decided to change the former rules of the club to the

"RUGBY" rules, and to commence play on Saturday afternoon next. The club will play at the Rifle Barracks as usual. The officers of the club for 1870 consist of John Loft, Esq., President; Rev. J. Scott, Vice-President; E. Waltham, Captain; Mr. F. A. Scott, Treasurer; Mr. R. J. Wade, Secretary; and Messrs. C. B. Lambert, E. W. Harrison, R. Hodgson and W. H. H. Hutchinson, Committee.

Saturday, 12th November 1870.
The Hull and North Lincolnshire Times,

FOOTBALL - HULL v LOUTH — A match was played at Louth between these clubs on Saturday last, and after a well-contested game, which was, however, a little in favour of Hull, resulted in a draw, neither side securing a goal. The Hull club was not at all "at home" with the rules of the Louth club, which differ very much from their own. E. Waltham for Hull and Morton, for Louth, played very well.

Saturday, 3rd December 1870.
The Hull and North Lincolnshire Times,

FOOTBALL — On Saturday afternoon a match was played at the Rifle Barracks between the football club and the First East York, Rifle Volunteers. The volunteers, although assisted by several members of the club, were very weak and were easily defeated, a goal being kicked by E. Waltham, from a touchdown by W. Hodgson, and another was soon obtained by G. E. Bennett. Sides were then chosen by E. Waltham and C. B. Lambert, and an exciting game was kept up until dark, resulting in the victory of Mr. Waltham's party by two goals, both obtained by R. J. Wade, to none. Owing to the Louth Football Club not being able to visit next Saturday, there will only be the usual practice in the afternoon.

Saturday, 25th February 1871.
The Hull and North Lincolnshire Times,

FOOTBALL — LEEDS v HULL — On Saturday a match was played between the clubs of these two towns at Ferriby, near Hull. The Leeds team mustered only nine, against the fifteen of Hull. The deficiency was, however, made up by three members of the Hull team kindly volunteering their services. This of course made the numbers up to twelve on a side. The game was commenced by a kick off from Hull, against wind and hill. Despite these disadvantages they managed to push their opponenets hard, and succeeded in getting a touch down. The try at goal, however, resulted in a failure. When time was called the goals were changed, and shortly, after an obstinate scrimmage, R. Butler touched the ball in their opponents' goal. Griesbach was deputed to take the kick, Gibson placing the ball. A judicious kick resulted in a goal. On this, of course, the goals were again changed, but no decided advantage was gained on either side. The match thus proved a victory for Leeds by one goal. On the Leeds side the following players did good service: Wright (the captain), Bradley (umpire), Brown, A. O. Butler, R. Butler, Gibson, Griesbach, Sykes and Wheatley.

In 1872 Hull became one of the first clubs in the North of England to join the English Rugby Union.

Members of the club around this time were the Hodgsons (William, Richard, Edward and Arthur), the Harrisons (Gilbert, Walter and Brian), F. Moss, E. W. Wade, Darbyshire, Norman and Salmon. In the first Yorkshire county match against Lancashire at Leeds, Hull had four members of the team, Waltham, Wood, Lambert and Hutchinson. The club's first colours were striped scarlet and white jersey, white cap (if any) and white flannels with the city's Three Crowns in a black badge on the jersey. Later, a move was made to a ground at the Haworth Arms field in Newland and when Huddersfield were the visitors, there were just twenty spectators! E. W. Wade kicked a late goal to give Hull victory. Both teams scored nine tries apiece.

Saturday, 25th April 1874.
The Hull and North Lincolnshire Times,

FOOTBALL — HULL v LEEDS — A match was played on Saturday on the ground of the Hull club, when the home team won by a goal. The following are the names of the players:- Leeds: Messrs. B. Cariss (captain), Crawfurd, D. Brown, J. Tennant, B. Hirst, J. Smith, A. Hill, W. Wrightson, C. E. Pease, J. Ogden, H. Myers, A. Gordon, and Christison. Hull: Messrs. E. Hodgson, R. Hodgson, Sharp, Hollingbury, Burton, B. Lambert (captain), W. H. Hutchinson, C. Bethell, S. Moss, Banister, W. Harrison, R. Wade, E. Wade, and G. Harrison.

Saturday, 11th November 1876.
The Hull and North Lincolnshire Times,

under SPORTS and PASTIMES. On Saturday a trial match between 15 Leeds and Hull and 15 of Bradford and York, for the Yorkshire team to be pitted against the Durham team in a match at Leeds next Saturday, was played in the Holbeck Recreation Grounds. The ball was kicked up off at three o'clock, and during the match, which ended in one goal at each side, some good play was manifested by Garnett (Bradford), Mills (Bradford), Tetley (Bradford), Seaton (Leeds), Shutt (Bradford), Christison (York), Hutchinson (Hull), Richardson (Bradford) and others.

Saturday, 25th November 1876.
The Hull and North Lincolnshire Times,

under SPORTS and PASTIMES. A match between the Hull and Bradford football clubs was played on Saturday on the ground of the former on the Anlaby road. The attendance of spectators was fair, although the weather was anything but favourable. The ground was very heavy, and many of the combatants suffered in consequence. Mr. Lambert officiated as umpire for both sides. The visitors won the toss, and it was soon apparent that the home team had met their equal, for the play had not continued many minutes before Bradford secured a touch. When, however, the ball was kicked for goal, it struck the crossbar, and the home team, under Mr. Hutchinson, making a good charge, it was some time before Bradford again secured a touch down. Again they failed to secure a goal, and Hull soon after succeeded in also getting a touch down. The play on both sides was very good, and the game was so hotly contested that when time was called neither party had won a goal, and the game terminated in favour of Bradford, who had scored three touches against their opponents one.

Saturday, 9th December 1876.
The Hull and North Lincolnshire Times,

under SPORTS and PASTIMES. A football match was played on Saturday between the Leeds and Hull Football Clubs. The weather was unfavourable. The Hull players won by two goals and one try, the visitors, though evidently pretty good players, securing neither element of victory in their favour. The following are the names of the teams:- Leeds — back, E. A. Mathews; three-quarter back, P. Cariss; half-backs, H. S. Manning (captain) and E. A. Seaton; forwards, Oct, Leatham, A. T. Holmes, E. Holwell, P. B. Wilkinson, J. C. Sykes, J. P. Sykes, G. M. Stewart, J. C. Atkinson, W. J. Hebblethwaite, and H. P. Furby. One of this team was unavoidably absent. Hull — backs, Backworth and E. Hodgson; three-quarter back, R. Hodgson; forwards, W. H. H. Hutchinson (captain), Lambert, G. Harrison, B. Harrison, N. P. Dobre, R. Deunett, E. T. Wise, W. H. Carr, and E. A. Wade.

Saturday, 31st March 1877.
The Hull and North Lincolnshire Times,

under SPORTS and PASTIMES. A match of football was played on Saturday between the Hull and Wakefield clubs, on the ground of the former, Anlaby Road. After some pretty good play the match terminated in favour of Hull by one goal, one try and three touches down. The following were the players on the respective sides, viz:- Hull — forwards, W. H. H. Hutchinson (captain), G. Harrison, F. Lambert, G. Wise, A. L. Bannister, A. Fisher, A. Dannatt, N. F. Dobree, and A. Beamont; backs, A. Hodgson and E. Hodgson; three-quarter backs, R. Hodgson and S. Silvester; half-backs, W. Hodgson and E. W. Harrison. Umpire — C. N. Lambert. Wakefield — forwards, C. H. Ward, C. Fernandez, G. Fernandez, H. Witham, E. Pickersgill, B. Kilner, H. Green, C. E. Peake and G. Knowles; backs, P. Lee and E. Stonehouse; quarter-backs, R. Holiday and F. Lee.

Hull were now considered to be among the strongest sides in Yorkshire in 1877, and when the Yorkshire Challenge Cup was introduced in that year, they were favourites to win "t'owd tin pot", but York beat them in the semi-finals. Representative honours came to Hull when Gilbert Harrison was chosen to play for England seven times between 1877 and 1885. New members included J. H. Hodge (Secretary), W. Vassall and H. F. Lowe (from Cheltenham), E. T. Wise (Treasurer) and W. J. Tall (from Rugby), W. S. Beaumont (from St. Peter's, York) plus David Wilson, A. Thorney, Thompson, Brough, Plaxton, W. J. Close, A. W. Lambert, H. Tall, A. Smithson, A. H. Tyacke, J. L. Read, R. E. Denett, J. C. Shears, West, Joy, Bethell, H. Williams and W. Calvert. Only sixteen members were actively involved on the playing side, and great difficulty was met in raising teams for away fixtures. Ten matches were played, five won, two lost and three drawn.

There were thirty playing members in season 1878/9 when nine matches were won, two lost and one drawn. Secretary H. F. Lowe announced "a team list can be viewed on Wednesday evening at the Imperial Hotel, Paragon Street" and "Club jerseys are available from Harland and Co. of Silver Street". Mr. Lowe's office was at 19 Parliament Street. Interest in rugby grew in 1879 and with forty-five playing members, a second team was formed. Thirteen first team matches were played, six won, four lost and three drawn. Hull were now playing on Anlaby Road, where West Park is now situated.

W. H. H. Hutchinson was born in Cottingham in 1849 and lived at Cottingham Hall. He attended Rugby school and played regularly in twenty-a-side games. He became a shipowner in Hull and remembered early matches for Hull: "Players unaware of the rules would grab my hair when I charged past them."

"In a match for Yorkshire against Lancashire, several Sheffield players, also with little knowledge of the rules, did not like the hard tackling of a Lancashire forward and one of the Sheffield men grabbed the ball by the lace and hammered his opponent about the head with it. I had to tell him it was not provided for in the rules and he seemed surprised to learn it!" Hutchinson played twice for England. Gibson scored five tries, Lovell three goals and Wilson two goals. Over five hundred miles were travelled to six away matches and home gates of 500 were reported. A balance of £4.9s.4d. was announced. Club jerseys could also be obtained from Maw Till Kirk Co. of Bridge Street.

Saturday, 22nd March 1879.
The Hull and North Lincolnshire Times,

HULL FOOTBALL CLUB — In the presence of a large number of spectators, the members of this club contested a match on Saturday on the Anlaby Road ground, between teams raised by J. C. Shears and E. T. Wise, the result of which was a victory for the former. The score was 5 tries, 4 touchdowns against 3 tries, 2 touchdowns. For the losers, Hodge, Lowe, Dennett, English and Wise were conspicuous; while for the winners, Robinson, Vassall, Beaumont, the two Birds, and Shears did all the work. The following are the teams:- 1st C. M. Wawm, back; W. Beaumont, half-back; W. Vassall and J. C. Shears, quarter-backs; E. Robinson, C. V. Bird, E. Bird, J. R. Read (captain), H. Williams, W. Dean, J. Dysart, and W. Wood, forwards. 2nd. H. F. Lowe, J. W. Thompson, three-quarter backs; R. E. Dennett, J. H. Hodge, half-backs; E. T. Wise (captain), P. English, F. Bolton, A. B. Priest, H. W. Stork, Thorpe, and Clarke forwards.

Saturday, 25th October 1879.
The Hull and North Lincolnshire Times,

FOOTBALL — MALTON v HULL — On Thursday an interesting match was played on Town's Pasture, Malton between these clubs. It was the first match of the season for the home club, and ended in their favour after sharp and close play, the teams being level. Malton kicked off, and in the first half pressed the visitors closely. At the close of the match, Malton were three touches down, two touches in goal, and one try, and Hull were eight touches down, and two touches in goal. The teams were:- Malton — Fred Waud (captain), Alfred Ezard, George Simpson, Ramsden Walker, E. Wright, James Hartley, C. Robson, Grundon, Smallwood (forwards), Joshua Hartley, F. Hartley (half-backs), F. Wadge and A. Wilson (three-quarter backs). Hull — W. G. Close, A. Gibson, G. Weetson, P. Dickenson, A. H. Tyacke, L. Whitehead, H. Roberts, C. H. Mawer, J. Hawthorne (forwards), E. Braithwaite, J. Douglas (half-backs), G. A. Hoskins (captain and three-quarter back), D. Lovell (back).

Saturday, 17th April 1880.
The Hull and North Lincolnshire Times,

HULL FOOTBALL CLUB — Last match of the season, played on the Anlaby Road ground, between the past and present members of the club. Teams: Past — E. Hodgson, R. Hodgson, A. Hodgson, B. Harrison, E. W. Harrison, F. B. Moss, W. Hodgson, B. Lambert, J. S. Moss, R. J. Wade, E. A. Wade, F. Hutchinson, F. F. Lambert, and D. N. Salmond. Present — T. W. Holdich, D. Lovell, L. Harrison, E. Robinson, B. Mackay, J. Thompson, R. Cooper, G. Harrison, E. Robinson, J. H. Hodge, E. T. Wise, L. C. Smith, J. L. Read, W. J. Tall, W. Bird, W. J. Close.

Hull had lost twice to a junior club, Hull White star, in the 1880/1 season and Hull's secretary, J. H. Hodge put a resolution to his members "that this club cease to exist, subject to the Hull White Star club taking our name and our members without ballot", and at the same time, Hull White Star resolved to "change our name to Hull Football Club and to admit all members of the late Hull Football Club". Both clubs passed these resolutions. 18 matches were played, 8 were won, 6 lost and 4 drawn.

FOOTBALL
HULL FOOTBALL CLUB — LIST OF ENGAGEMENTS 1880.
FIRST XV

November 20 — Bradford .... Bradford
      "   27 — St. Peter's .... York
December 4 — Halifax .... Halifax
      "   11 — Gainsborough .... Hull
      "   18 — Dewsbury Shamrocks .... Dewsbury
    8   27 — Leeds Rovers .... Hull
January   1 — Leeds .... Leeds
      "   8 — Selby .... Selby
      "   13 — Malton .... Malton
      "   15 — Dewsbury Shamrocks .... Hull
      "   22 — White Star .... Hull
      "   29 — Goole .... Hull
February 5 — Leeds Rovers .... Leeds
      "   12 — Halifax .... Hull
      "   19 — Scarborough .... Scarborough
      "   26 — Harrogate .... Hull
March   5 — Bingley (challenge cup) .... Hull
      "   12 — Bradford Rangers .... Hull
      "   19 — Goole .... Goole
      "   26 — Scarborough .... Hull

SECOND XV

November 20 — Club Game .... Hull
      "   27 — Selby .... Hull
December 4 — Club Game .... Hull
      "   11 — Club Game .... Hull
      "   18 — Dewsbury Shamrocks .... Hull
      "   27 — Club Game .... Hull
January   1 — Southcoates .... Hull
      "   8 — Club Game .... Hull
      "   15 — Dewsbury Shamrocks .... Dewsbury
      "   22 — White Star .... White Star
      "   29 — Newington .... Newington
February 5 — Dock Company .... Hull
      "   12 — Gainsborough .... Gainsborough
      "   19 — Scarborough .... Hull
      "   26 — Club Game .... Hull
March   5 — Leeds .... Hull
      "   12 — Club Game .... Hull
      "   19 — Club Game .... Hull
      "   26 — Scarborough .... Scarborough

Saturday, 13th November 1880.
The Hull and North Lincolnshire Times,

HULL SOUTHCOATES v HULL (SECOND ELEVEN) — These clubs met on the former's ground on Saturday, and a good and well-contested game ended in favour of the Southcoates Club by 4 tries and 11 touches down to Hull's 1 touch down. The tries were got by Douglas, Longbottom, Thompson, and Ramsden (one each). Stancer and Wooton, in addition to those named, played hard and well, whilst Harrison and Wawn, for Hull, were the most prominent of a good team. Players:- Southcoates — W. Tomlinson (back), J. Douglas (captain), T. Lofthouse (three-quarter back), W. Lane and J. E. Stancer (half-backs), J. Wooton, W. Thompson, W. Hodge, C. Owen, R. Henderson, J. Rundell, J. T. Longbottom, A. Ramsden, B. Hood and Coates (forwards). Hull — Wawn (back), L. Harrison, H. Tall (three-quarter backs), J. Downs, B. M. Mackay (half-backs), P. English, H. Downs, J. Elsworth, W. Smithson, A. E. Mason, H. T. Smith, Haigh, R. Simpson, and Reckitt (forwards). Hull played 14 men only.

Saturday, 13th November 1880.
The Hull and North Lincolnshire Times,

HARROGATE v HULL — This match was played on Saturday at Harrogate. There was a good attendance of spectators. A fast game ensued, and for some time neither side gained the advantage, but Wells securing the ball, made a capital run, and secured a try for Harrogate. The kick at goal was a failure, but immediately after Wells dropped a beautiful goal from the field of play. On changing ends the game for a time was most evenly contested, until Dobson by a long run got into the Hull lines, and shortly after followed this up with a second try. Stephenson kicked a goal from the place, and after a fine bit of play, Longhorne secured another try. When time was called the game stood — Harrogate, two goals, three tries, nine touch-downs, and a dead ball to nil. Players:- Harrogate — Brown, back; Langhorne and Wells (captain), three-quarter backs; Dobson and Horner, half-backs; F. W. Fletcher, T. Harper, J. Pearson, Brown, Wainwright, Gospel, Appleton, J. Hudson, and M. Stephenson, forwards. Hull (14) — T. W. Holdich, back; E. Robinson, W. J. Fall, and R. R. Hutchinson, three-quarter backs; J. H. Hodge and A. Smithson, half-backs; Gossage, Selkirk, W. G. Jackson, H. F. Lowe, J. L. Read, H. Palent, H. J. Smith, and O. Smith, forwards.

Saturday, 4th December 1880.
The Hull and North Lincolnshire Times,

SELBY v HULL — This match was played on Saturday when the Selby team journeyed to Hull, the weather being all that could be deemed for the occasion. The captain won the toss, and chose to defend the town goal. The Hull (second team) kicked off, and the ball was at once returned by Chambers, the forwards at once following up and compelling the home team to touch-down twice in quick succession. Shortly after Townend got the ball, and ran in from the half-way flag and gained a try, from which Upton landed a goal. Hull kicking from the half-way flag, the leather was again returned into the home quarters, and another try was got, from which Pruss kicked a goal. Half-time being called, the Selby captain kicked off and fast and loose scrimmages took place. The Hull team now obtained three tries. Selby now seeing how matters stood made another effort, and obtained a third try; but this was not to be the last, as Fennell and Eccles obtained a fourth try, which Upton converted into a goal. Shortly after this Selkirk, getting on the ball, made a good dribble, and forced Selby to save. Darkness now coming on and time being up, the game was brought to a termination in the centre of the field. Score:- Selby three goals, one try, and five touch-downs to Hull three tries, and one touch-down. Teams:-Hull — Warne, back; Smith, Priest (captain), and Morton, three-quarter backs; R. R. Hutchinson and A. Smithson, half-backs; J. L. Read, A. Reckitt, Elsworth, Mooney, Selkirk, C. Read, forwards. Selby-A —Chambers and C. Pruss, backs; E. P. Upton (captain), and H. Townend, three-quarter backs; G. H. Jones and J. Briggs, half-backs; F. Sefton, J. C. Fennell, J. Bradley, J. Palfrey, Parker, C. Connell, Eccles, and J. Keogh, forwards.

Saturday, 12th March 1881.
The Hull and North Lincolnshire Times,

FOOTBALL

THE YORKSHIRE CHALLENGE CUP TIE — BINGLEY v HULL — The Rugby Union game was in Yorkshire at the zenith of its glory on Saturday afternoon last, the occasion being the first round of the challenge cup ties, which proved an immense success, many thousands of spectators —nearly 10,000 at Dewsbury alone — witnessing the various games. At Hull the home team was matched against Bingley, and the play resulted in an easy win for the visitors. Wilkinson kicked off for Bingley, and the ball being well followed up, the first scrimmage being formed in the home half, and they were soon compelled to touch-down twice. From the drop out Dawson secured the first try for Bingley, which failed. Soon after Hoskins made a good dribble, and the home team had to touch-down several times in quick succession. On change of ends, Thompson kicked off, but Wilkinson returned well, and the home team had to again "save". Soon after Dawson got possession, and, passing the whole of the home players, secured the second try for Bingley, but Wilkinson failed to place it. Time was soon after called, leaving Bingley winners by two tries and ten touch-downs to one touch-down. Teams: Hull — Hutchinson, Vassell, R. Brough, F. Brough, Thompson, Harrison, Hoskins, Smith, Lambert, Tall, Hodge, Robinson, Tall, Read, and Morton. Bingley — E. Wilkinson, J. Hastings, C. Hanson, J. Dawson, T. Wood, H. Wright, J. Gott, S. Walker, J. Foulds, S. Asquith, W. Asquith, I. Foulds, J. Crowther, J. L. Hickson, and O. Preston. During the match, and shortly before half-time, a lamentable accident occurred. Brough, one of the Hull team, made an attempt to kick the ball, and missing it, kicked one of the visitors named Wright so severely that the right leg was broken. Dr. Atkinson was fortunately on the field, and after examination ordered the injured man to be at once taken to the Infirmary, where his leg was subsequently dressed, and he is now progressing favourably.

THE HULL FOOTBALL CLUB
Air — "A fine old English Gentleman".

We sometimes hear that Englishmen are going down the hill,
That in sport, and on the battlefield we've lost both nerve and will,
My song is of a mimic strife and deny it he who can,
That of the games of Britons, Rugby football leads the van.
CHORUS — Ho a jolly band of players, are the roving H.F.C.

In the Shire of broad acres, are many famous cracks,
From farfamed Wakefield Trinity, Bradford, Leeds and Halifax,
Bold Thornes, and many a plucky team descendant of John Bull,
But a Club to one day win the Cup, hails from the Town of Hull.
CHORUS — Ho a jolly band etc.

They fearlessly the pick of Yorkshire Football Clubs have faced,
Tho' often beaten in the field, have never been disgraced,
And of the men who've scored her well, I'll try to tell in rhyme,
I ask patience till "no side" for now we've reached "half-time".
CHORUS — Ho a jolly band etc.

Will Calvert, Captain of the team, no courage does he lack.
Fleet of foot, and steady nerve, a sure three-quarter back,
And next, a football pioneer, who's helped the Club to fame,
Here's a health to G. A. HOSKINS, football, and play the game.
CHORUS — Ho a jolly band etc.

The Brothers Braithwaite, George & Ted, have done their share of work,
And demon Smith, and sturdy Belt, were never known to shirk,
With Lovell stood between the posts, to kick the ball or run,
And the coming men are Smithsons, who with James will be A.1.
CHORUS — Ho a jolly band etc.

And now line up you forwards, just hear a word from me,
Close, Wilson, Winter and Lars Smith, with our reckless friend J.C.
And dashing Tyacke and Whitehead, you must all put archer up,
We'll give you hearty welcome with the Yorkshire Challenge Cup.
CHORUS — Ho a jolly band etc.

———————————

A song sheet issued around this time.

Chapter Three
HULL WHITE STAR

Hull White Star's history started in 1873 when a rugby team, called Albert played on Todd's Field on Sutton Bank as did a side named Zingari, whose members were mainly cricketers They formed the White Star Cricket Club in the summer and in turn they formed the Hull White Star Football Club. The club's first secretary was W. J. Close and treasurer Charles Brewer, who was also a half-back and topped the try scoring list one season. Mr. Brewer later became President of Hull F.C.

White Star played under association football rules with Lincolnshire clubs and rugby with a few Yorkshire teams. Their playing strip was firstly a blue and white jersey and later a black jersey with a white star emblazoned on the chest, black knickers and black stockings. They rented a ground on David Pearson's field, Sweet Dews Farm, behind the Anti-Mill on Holderness Road in 1875 and played matches against Gainsborough (celebrating afterwards at the White Hart, Gainsborough) and against Brigg (followed by a visit to The Angel Hotel, Brigg). Eleven matches were completed in 1877 including fixtures against Hull seconds, York Amateurs, Selby and Market Rasen. A new ground had been taken on Hall's Field, further along Holderness Road. The rent was £4.00 in the first season and secretary W. J. Close recalled later that at the first club match when gate money was taken, it amounted to 2/6d. and match expenses were 3/6d! Later gate receipts included 14/- v Brigg; £1.14s. v Ossett; 9/3d. v Stanley; 15/10d. v Southcoates; £2.6s. v Barnsley; 10/2d. v Malton; £2.8s.3d. v Gainsborough; £4.15s.4½d. v Hull and £3.8s.2½d. v York. The first West Riding club to be played was Kirkstall. Members around this time included, P. Dickinson, G. W. Braithwaite, T. Sparrow, S. Bell, C. Lightowler, C. H. Mawer, F. Mawer, W. J. Close, T. Adams, J. Wilkins, G. A. Hoskins, C. Whitehead, T. Harrison, E. M. Braithwaite and F. R. Helman.

Saturday, 23rd December 1876.
The Hull and North Lincolnshire Times,

under SPORTS and PASTIMES — A football match was played on Saturday between Brigg and White Star of Hull, on the Holderness Road and resulted in a victory for the home team, they having scored two goals, four tries, and several touch-downs to "love". The tries and goals were obtained by the following players: George Watson and W. Brewer, two tries; H. Pearson and Thos. Harrison, one try; P. Dickinson and G. Hoskins (captain) kicked goals. The following were players for the White Star, George Hoskins (captain), C. Brewer, half-backs; George Braithwaite, three-quarter back; J. Wilson, back; P. Dickinson, W. Close, T. Harrison, G. Watson, E. Braithwaite and F. Mawer, forwards.

Saturday, 12th October 1878.
Hull and North Lincolnshire Times,

SPORTS and PASTIMES — FOOTBALL — HULL WHITE STAR — The opening match of this club was played on Saturday afternoon on their new ground, Holderness Road, before a large company of spectators. The ground was in first-class condition, and although a little further from the town, is an improvement on the old one. The teams raised by the captain, Mr. Hoskins, and Mr. Wilson met, when after an hour and a half's good hard play, victory fell to Mr. Wilson's team by one try and three touchdowns to one touchdown. Some of the older members were greatly missed, chiefly W. Close and Pearson, two very good forwards, and Wilkins, a useful half-back, who are not playing this season; but the club have a good acquisition of new men, some of whom look likely to

George A. Hoskins.

make good players. Home-and-away matches are arranged with the first fifteens of Hull, Kirkstall, Malton, Gainsborough, York Amateurs, and Lees Blenheim; an annual match with Mirfield, and a scratch twelve play Association rules against Brigg. The club is also entered for the Yorkshire Challenge Cup, and the season promises to be a most successful one.

Saturday, 22nd March 1879.
The Hull and North Lincolnshire Times,

FOOTBALL — HULL WHITE STAR v GAINSBOROUGH — The return match between these two clubs was played on Saturday afternoon, on the ground of the former, Holderness Road, Hull. A very hard fought and pleasant game resulted in a victory for the home team by four tries and eight touches-down, to Gainsborough nil. The tries were obtained by Brewer, Mawer, Watson, and Douglas, who played well, as also did Hoskins, Dickinson, Burton, Elmhurst, Rimmington, and Handisides for their respective teams. The following were the players:- Hull — Hoskins (captain), Brewer, Close, Dickinson, Sparrow, Mawer, Watson, Wilson, Douglas, Braithwaite, Bell and Walker. Gainsborough — Elmhurst (captain), Burton, Rimmington, Mackay, Barnes, Holt, Sparrow, Wileman, Handisides, Birkett, Mansfield and Gibson.

HULL WHITE STAR F.C. – Season 1879-1880
Back Row: C. A. Brewer (Hon. Treas.), E. M. Braithwaite, B. R. Wilson,
G. G. Watson, W. Gibson, L. Whitehead, F. L. Mawer, C. H. Mawer,
G. W. Braithwaite.
Middle Row: P. E. Dickinson, W. H. Ellis (President), S. Bell.
In Front: J. Douglas, W. Close (Hon. Sec.), J. C. Lightowler, G. A. Hoskins (Capt.),
T. Harrison, H. Roberts, T. Sparrow.

Saturday, 24th January 1880.
The Hull and North Lincolnshire Times,

FOOTBALL — HULL WHITE STAR v YORK MELBOURNE — These clubs played a match on the York ground on Saturday. York kicked off. Both sides scored three touchdowns each. The following were the players:- Hull — D. Lovell, B. Wilson, backs; G. A. Hoskins (captain), G. W. Braithwaite, three-quarter backs; T. Harrison, L. Whitehead, half-backs; P. Dickinson, A. Gibson, C. H. Mawer, F. Mawer, T. Sparrow, E. Braithwaite, G. Watson, T. Marshall, and W. J. Cleave, forwards. York — G. Miller, back; W. Heptage, F. Birch three-quarter backs; H. Curtis, G. Holder, half-backs; H. Gill, F. Cass, E. Jefferson, J. Oxberry, H. Passmore, A. Sawyers, B. Taylor, W. Redpath, E. Curtis, and H. Bean (captain), forwards.

Saturday, 6th March 1880.
The Hull and North Lincolnshire Times,

FOOTBALL — HULL WHITE STAR v BARNSLEY — White Star:- B. Wilson, back; G. W. Braithwaite and W. Calvert, three-quarter backs; Kennington and C. A. Brewer, half-backs; G. A. Hoskins (captain), E. Braithwaite, F. Mawer, P. Dickinson, H. L. Smith, L. Whitehead, T. Sparrow, A. Gibson, T. Harrison and W. J. Close forwards; Mr. Roberts, umpire.

25

Saturday, 9th October 1880.
The Hull and North Lincolnshire Times,

HULL WHITE STAR FOOTBALL CLUB — The members of this club having had several practice games since the beginning of September, opened the season on Saturday afternoon by playing a match, "first fifteen" v "next twenty", on their old ground, Holderness Road. The result was a decided victory for the "fifteen", but although the "twenty" only scored a minor point or two, they contested the game well, and by the form displayed by some of the juniors, it is evident that the club will be able to keep up its old prestige. The list of fixtures for the coming season is the best the club has yet had, there being the first fifteen home and away matches with Barnsley, Hull, Heckmondwike, Kirkstall, Ossett, York Melbourne, Bradford, Zingari, &c, while the second team play the first teams of Newington, Southcoates, Dock Company, and the second teams of Hull and York Melbourne. Next Saturday afternoon the first team meet Barnsley on the Holderness Road ground, and a very good game is expected.

Saturday, 13th November 1880.
The Hull and North Lincolnshire Times,

HULL WHITE STAR v KIRKSTALL — This match was played on the Holderness Road ground, Hull, on Saturday afternoon, before a large number of spectators. The visitors arrived in the town about twelve o'clock, but were late in turning up at the ground, and the game was not started until 3.40, nearly an hour after the advertised time. Kirkstall kicked off, and by following up well kept the ball in the home team's quarters, where it remained for some time, and scrimmage after scrimmage was formed. At length Denehey got possession, crossed the line, and gained a try in fine style; from this Kirkstall kicked a goal. The ball was re-statrted from the centre by Hull, and from now up to the call of time, the play was very fast, and needs little description, as neither side scored beyond touch downs, Hull gaining four to Kirkstall one. A few minutes before time was called the visitors played up most resolutely to gain some further advantage, when a long drop kick by one of their backs was not returned, and being well followed up, a try was obtained close to the touch line. The ball was brought out and placed as for the kick at goal, but instead of doing this, Broadhead kicked to Cookson, who picked the ball up, made a splendid run, and gained another try, from which the same player kicked a goal. White Star started the ball again, and at once carried it across the Kirkstall line, but only a touch down resulted. Time was now called, the score standing, Kirkstall two goals, one try, and two touch downs, to Hull six touch downs. Teams: Hull —D. Lovell, back; G. W. Braithwaite, B. R. Wilson, three-quarter backs; C. A. Brewer, G. Kennington, F. Jones, half-backs; G. A. Hoskins (captain), W. J. Close, A. H. Tyacke, C. H. Mawer, L. Whitehead, T. Sparrow, E. M. Braithwaite, H. L. Smith, L. Butler, forwards. Kirkstall — A. D. Summerscales, back; A. Hoyle, A. Mason, three-quarter backs; M. G. Mather, J. W. Speight, J. C. Broadhead (captain), half-backs; F. Cookson, H. Walker, S. Pitt, D. S. Denehey, S. Speight, W. Peat, J. Witham, S. Bell, H. Roberts, forwards.

Saturday, 4th December 1880.
The Hull and North Lincolnshire Times,

HULL WHITE STAR v EARLE'S ENGINEERS — On Saturday afternoon a match was played on the Holderness Road ground between a scratch team of the White Star Club and 16 players (under the captaincy of H. L. Smith) connected with Messrs. Earle's works. The game was very fast and well contested, but the Engineers were over-matched in speed, and when time was called they had not scored, while the club team had obtained two tries and six minor points. Hoskins gained the tries in fine style, and played remarkably well throughout. Smith, Tyacke, Whitehead, and Braithwaite also showed good form. Teams: Earle's (16) — Lovell, back; Sparrow, Morgan, three-quarter backs; Smith, Roberts, half-backs; Tyacke, Walker, Coulson, Pound, Eldridge, Shaw, Turner, Lison, Dearden, Hewitt, and Shaw, forwards. White Star — Eccles, back; Hoskins (captain), Braithwaite, half-backs; Whitehead, Mawer, Hart, Winter, Heaton, Butler, Hewitt, Jones, Hebron, forwards.

Thursday, 7th April 1881.
The Hull and Eastern Counties Herald,

HULL v HULL WHITE STAR — The return match was played on the ground of the former on Saturday. There was a large attendance of spectators. White Star kicked off, the ball was well returned, and Hull, following up at once, carried the game to the visitors' line, who, to relieve their side, promptly touched town. After the drop out play became very fast, but was chiefly confined to the forwards, Robinson, L. Smith, Mawer, Womack, and Winter being very conspicuous. White Star now pressed the home team, and Dickinson crossed their line, but the try was not allowed; the ball was scrimmaged near the goal line. Hull worked it away a few yards, but on becoming loose, H. Smith got possession, and, lashing through the Hull men, gained a try, the shot at goal by Lovell only scored a touch down. Hull now tried hard to get away, Brough and Chubley putting in some useful runs and kicks, but Lovell always returned into touch in the home "twenty-five". Several scrimmages ensued, Hull having to touch down three times in quick succession. This brought about half-time. The game was at once re-started by Hull, and the backs got a little more to do, Hoskins, G. Braithwaite, L. Harrison, and F. Brough making several short runs, but the tackling on both sides was very good, which prevented them getting down. The ball was now worked into the visitors' "twenty-five", where Kennington got possession, made a short run, and then passed to Wilson, who made the run of the day, and got a try in fine style. The place kick was again a failure. The Hull men played into the hands of F. Brough, and he tried hard to get away, but was well looked after by E. Braithwaite, Womack, and Mawer. Two fair catches were made by Wilson. The kicks by Hoskins, although very good ones, only registered touch downs. From a kick out H. Smith ran in again, but the try was objected to, and the point was waived. Chubley now had the misfortune to injure his leg, and had to be removed from the field. Shortly after "No side" was called, the score standing — White Star two tries and ten touch downs, to Hull's one touch down. Teams: Hull — Wawn, back; Chubley, F. Brough,

L. Harrison, three-quarter backs; Hutchinson, Smithson, half-backs; J. Robinson (captain), J. H. Hodge, N. Brough, A. Lambert, L. Smith, H. Tall, J. W. Tall, Cooper, and J. L. Read, forwards. White Star — D. Lovell, back; G. Braithwaite, B. Wilson, and G. A. Hoskins (captain), three-quarter backs; H. Smith, G. Kennington, half-backs; F. Mawer, J. Womack, T. Harrison, E. Braithwaite, L. Whitehead, A. H. Tyacke, P. E. Dickinson, T. Sparrow, and F. Winter, forwards.

Chapter Four
AMALGAMATION

On the fusion of the two clubs, new team colours were introduced, a black jersey with the Three Crowns emblem in blue and gold on the chest but later a change back to cherry and white stripes was made. However it was discovered that these two colours "ran" when washed and the club reverted back to black jerseys with white knickers, hence the nickname "The All-Blacks" in the late 1880's/early 1890's. The ground at Holderness Road (on land where Mersey and Severn Streets now stand) could hold 2,500 in two stands covered with a corrugated iron roof and 2,500 at the two ends. There was a four foot high fence around the playing area, large shields with coat of arms on the goal lines and the centre line. The 25 yard lines were marked with large shields and a large board on the front of one covered stand near its roof informed the crowd of the length of time over which the game was to be played. There were three turnstiles and admission was 3d. The "amalagamation" proved a real shot in the arm for rugby in Hull and the East Riding and membership on the playing side quickly grew to eighty-six.

The first officers of the club were W. Ellis (President), G. A. Hoskins (captain), Vice-Presidents, Dr. Holder, E. Atkin, G. W. Braithwaite, Treasurer, F. Tindle and Hon. Secretary, W. J. Close. Matches were played in Yorkshire, Lancashire, Durham and Northumberland, and short tours of the U.K. were undertaken.

A sum of £2.8s.5d. was spent on advertising the change of name to those concerned with rugby union. Nine players had won their county caps — G. Jacketts, W. Calvett, G. Belt, F. L. Mawer, E. Coulman, H. Simpson, A. P. Iveson, W. Teal and H. J. W. Oxlade.

Saturday, 8th October 1881.
The Hull and North Lincolnshire Times,

HULL FOOTBALL CLUB — An account of a match on the Holderness Road ground between the first fifteen and the second twenty. Teams: First Fifteen — L. Butler, F. Jones, B. R. Wilson, G. A. Hoskins (captain), H. J. Smith, J. Womack, A. H. Tyacke, W. J. Close, H. Tall, W. S. Beaumont, E. Robinson, F. Winter, L. Whitehead. Second Twenty — M. Wawne, F. Tindle, Atkin, A. Smithson, S. Bell (captain), H. Roberts, W. Lison, F. Chaplin, T. Cook, J. Wilson, F. F. Curtis, A. Mason, J. H. Hodge, A. Mooney, P. H. Pease, C. H. Mawer, T. S. Twite, and four others.

Saturday, 10th December 1881.

HULL v KIRKSTALL — Exciting match,. Account of a match where Hull defeated Kirkstall, the first team to do so that season. At one point in the game the spectators invaded the pitch. Hull's team: D. R. Lovell, G. W. Braithwaite,

W. F. B. Calvert, G. A. Hoskins (captain), J. F. B. Calvert, W. J. Tall, L. Whitehead, E. Robinson, E. M. Braithwaite, L. Brown, and A. N. Other.

Saturday, 25th March 1882.
The Hull and North Lincolnshire Times,

HULL v LEEDS ST. JOHN — Hull: G. Kaye, G. W. Braithwaite, W. F. B. Calvert, G. A. Hoskins, G. E. Belt, H. L. Smith, E. M. Braithwaite, J. F. B. Calvert, W. J. Close, A. H. Tyacke (captain), E. Robinson, J. Womack, L. White-head and J. Wilson.

W. F. B. Calvert

The club's A.G.M. of 1881/2 was held at the Nags Head Inn on Holderness Road and it revealed that there were now 133 members, with nine matches won and fourteen lost. Fixtures had been played with Scarborough, Dewsbury Shamrocks, Salterhebble, Leeds St. John, York Melbourne, Ossett, York St. Peters and Kirkstall, among others. G. A. Hoskins was the leading try scorer with ten, and D. R. Lovell topped the goal kicking list. On 8th October, the team which played Scarborough away on the cricket field was: Lovell, Hoskins, Wilson, Smith, Smithson, Tyacke, Robinson, the Tall brothers, Beaumont, Braithwaite, Read, Winter, Close and Womack. Hull won by two goals to two tries, one try and eight touchdowns to one try and two touchdowns. The balance sheet recorded a season's gate money of £103 and £1.6s. spent on purchasing rugby balls. Nearly £41 went on travel by train to away matches. Sandwich board men had been used to advertise matches at a total cost of £3.12s.6d! The Directors of the club recommended that the players kept fit in the summer months by playing the Canadian game of La Crosse.

By 1882 the club was really thriving and seventy members were recruited, giving a total membership of 205. Braithwaite, Hewetson and Co. erected a stand, boarded in and fenced round for £131.17s.9d. Receipts included £308 taken in gate money and £11 rent received for grazing rights on the field! The average home gate was 3,000 while for the away match against Thornes, horses and rullies (carts) were hired to transport the team and officials at a cost of 8/6d. Lt. Col. Smith of Tranby Lodge, Hessle, presided over the club's A.G.M., held at the Hull Temperance Club in Albion Street, and among players who received special mention were G. Braithwaite, J. Calvert and

W. Calvert, F. Mawer, G. Hoskins and W. Tomlinson. Twenty-seven matches were played, eleven won, thirteen lost and three drawn. G. A. Hoskins scored seven tries and W. Tomlinson kicked six goals in his twenty-six appearances. It seemed that some members of the original Hull Club were conspicuous by their absence at the new club and they had preferred to 'join junior clubs in the area'. Over 1,700 miles were travelled to matches, including a short tour of the South of England in March. Seventeen members went and they received 30/-allowance and had their rail fares paid less 1/-, but they had to pay 5/- bed and breakfast per day themselves. The referee for the match against the Falcons at the Half Moon ground, Putney was Rowland Hill, Hon.Sec. of the Rugby Football Union and Hull won by two tries to nil. After the match "songs and recitations" were enjoyed after dinner at the Holborn Restaurant, High Holborn. After a day's rest, Clapham Rovers were the opposition at Wandsworth Common and the Yorkshiremen were victors again, this time by one goal, two tries and three minor points to four minor points.

In the away match against Goole earlier in the season, their opponents disputed one of the referee's decisions and walked off the field of play, causing the match to be abandoned.

Saturday 30th September 1882.
The Hull and North Lincolnshire Times,

HULL v WAKEFIELD TRINITY — Hull — D. Lovell, G. Braithwaite, W. Calvert (captain), R. James, J. Belt, H. L. Smith, J. Calvert, A. H. Tyacke, W. Winter, J. Wilson, L. Brown, W. Close, G. Hoskins, L. Whitehead, and E. Braithwaite.

Saturday, 21st October 1882.
The Hull and North Lincolnshire Times,

HULL v LONDON FALCONS — London Falcons' first match to be played in Yorkshire, they played Hull on the Holderness Road ground. Hull's team — W. Smithson, W. Calvert (captain), G. Braithwaite, W. Tomlinson, G. Hoskins, H. L.Smith, J. Calvert, J. R. James, L. Brown, L. Whitehead, W. J. Close, F. Winter. T. Cook. J. Wilson, A. H. Tyacke.

Saturday, 18th November 1882.
The Hull and North Lincolnshire Times,

THORNES v HULL — Hull's team: Tomlinson, Calvert (captain), Braithwaite, Hoskins, Smith, Braithwaite, Close, Calvert, Mawer, Shotton, Wilson, Winter, Tyacke, Read and Whitehead.

Saturday, 25th November 1882.
The Hull and North Lincolnshire Times,

YORKSHIRE v MIDLAND COUNTIES — Played at Wakefield, the Yorkshire side included W. F. B. Calvert, from Hull, playing as a three-quarter back.

HULL v OSSETT

HULL ('A' TEAM) v HULL CHURCH INSTITUTE — Hull's team: H. Aitkin, F. Winter, A. Thornton, H. Smith, S. Bell, J. Mooton G. Jacketts,

J. Kennington, T. Cook, A. W. Wade, W. H. Hodge, F. Johnson, F. Harrison, F. Tindle, and C. H. Edge.

W. J. Close resigned as secretary in 1883 after five years of service and at a dinner held in his honour at the Cross Keys Hotel, Market Place, he was presented with a solid silver tea and coffee service manufactured by Barnett and Scott of Hull. Mr. W. Hoskins, organist at St. James' Church, accompanied members on the piano. Fred Mawer was elected secretary in his place and the club captain was W. F. B. Calvert. Thirty-one matches were played, twelve won, fifteen lost and four drawn. The *Hull Times* instigated a Hull and District Rugby Union competition with a silver challenge trophy but the Hull first team was barred from entering to "equalise competition".

Three train loads of supporters followed the club to the Leeds St. John ground when Hull met Bradford in the Yorkshire Challenge Cup Final before a grand crowd of 15,000. Shortly before the kick-off, the Wellington Street area near to the ground was full of waggonettes, cabs and omnibuses but the match itself was a disappointment to the Hull fans. Their team's forwards played it tight but the backs were poor and Hull went down by one try to Bradford's four tries and one goal. Hull's team was — W. Tomlinson, G. Calvert, J. James, B. Wilson, G. Belt, H. Bell, W. Calvert (capt.) G. Harrison, C. Simpson, G. Jacketts, J. Wilson, J. Calvert, F. Mawer, W. Teal and L. Whitehead.

Umpires were T. Glover and B. Kilner while the referee was G. Thomson.

Fixtures during the season were arranged with Thornes, Manningham, Cleckheaton, Bingley and Horbury, among others. Larger crowds were being attracted and so a second grandstand was built to accommodate them and extensive work was carried out on pitch drainage. The yearly playing subscription was 5/-. Gilbert Harrison played for Yorkshire against Durham and Northumberland, and W. Calvert for Yorkshire against Cheshire and Oxford. A balance of £83.8s.5d. was reported and one item from the balance sheet was £16.6s. paid for referees' fees.

The club chairman in 1884 was Mr. F. Tindle, and Fred Mawer and Doug Boyd were joint secretaries. Yorkshire County honours came to F. Mawer, G. Belt, G. Harrison, W. Calvert and G. Jacketts. The club's membership was now

Bradford's Bonsor takes on Hull in the 1883 Yorkshire Cup Final at Leeds.

W. Teal.   Fred L. Mawer.

three hundred and twenty and three new turnstiles were constructed to cope
with increasing crowds. Thirty-four matches were played and nineteen were
won, twelve lost and three drawn. H. Bell was an ever-present, W. Calvert and
W. Teal were top try scorers and G. Jacketts was the leading goal kicker. The
club's A.G.M. was held at the Queens Hotel and members heard details of the
short tours of Lancashire and South Wales. Hire of buses from E. S. Annison
during the season amounted to £19.8s.6d. and a balance of £363 was
announced.

Bradford were unhappy at the injury to a player called Hawcridge and
refused to renew their fixture with Hull the next season "because of the general
rough and unscientific play of the Hull club."

Fixtures in 1885 included matches against Gala Melrose (Scotland),
Swansea, Hartlepool, Sheffield, Horbury and Llanelli. W. Calvert was top try
scorer with B. R. Wilson main goalkicker. Gilbert Harrison was selected as
captain of Yorkshire and E. Coulman and A. P. Iveson also played for their
county. President Lt. Col. Smith (late Scots Guards) told the club's A.G.M. at
the Public Rooms, Jarrett Street, that membership stood at four hundred and
sixty-eight and more construction work had to be carried out on the
grandstand. Sickness benefit of £1.10s. was payable to players unable to work
through injuries sustained playing rugby. Results — 31 played, won 17, lost 10,
drew 4.

Halifax Cricket and Football Club invited Hull to play the first rugby match
on their new enclosure in September 1886. G. Harrison and W. Teal played for

Yorkshire and Hull's playing record was fifteen wins, eleven defeats and four draws. W. Calvert (tries) and W. Kassell (goals) topped the scorers' lists and Calvert and F. Dickinson played in every match. Club caps were awarded to players after they had played thirty-five first team matches. The A.G.M. held at the Gladstone Hall, Bond Street, heard of athletic sports held at the ground during the summer.

The "A" team won the Hull and District Rugby Union Cup. J. C. Lightowler resigned as groundsman and J. Edson, former groundsman of Hull Town Cricket Club, replaced him. His wages were £63 for the season. The twelve acres of land which Hull rented at Holderness Road belonged to a Mr. Liddell, but as the tenure was due to be renewed, the club looked at other options. One was extensive land at Hull Botanic Gardens at Spring Bank when the company running the Gardens went into liquidation. However, despite lengthy negotiations to purchase the land and talk of joining up with Hull Cricket Club, who planned to move from their Asylum Lane ground, the asking price proved too high and Hull Corporation eventually sold the land to the founders of Hymers College.

FIRST FIFTEEN

Date			Club	Ground
1886	September	11	Opening Match	Home
	"	18	Halifax	Away
	"	25		Home
	October	2	Castleford	Away
	"	9	Leeds Parish Church	Home
	"	16	Oldham	Away
	"	23	Dewsbury	Home
	"	30		Away
	November	6	Manningham	Away
	"	13	York	Home
	"	20	Leeds Parish Church	Away
	"	27	Lansdowne (Dublin)	Home
	December	4	Hartlepool Rovers	Away
	"	6		Away
	"	7	West of Scotland	Away
	"	11	Salford	Home
	"	18	Rochdale Hornets	Away
	"	27	Clapham Rovers	Home
1887	January	1	Leeds St. John's	Away
	"	8	Hartlepool Rovers	Home
	"	15	Dewsbury	Away
	"	22	Leeds St. John's	Home
	"	29	Oldham	Home
	February	5	Manningham	Home
	"	12	York	Away
	"	19	Rochdale Hornets	Home
	"	26	Thornes (Y. C. Tie)	Home

FIRST FIFTEEN

Date			Club	Ground
1887	March	5	Thornes (Y. C. Tie)	
	"	12	"	
	"	19	"	
	"	26	"	
	April	2	Salford	Away
	"	9	Halifax	Home
	"	11	Castleford	Home
	"	16		Away

SECOND FIFTEEN

Date			Club	Ground
1886	September	11	Opening Match	Home
	"	18	Halifax	Home
	"	25	Sheffield	Away
	October	2	Castleford	Home
	"	9	Leeds Parish Church	Away
	"	16	Wakefield United	Home
	"	23	Dewsbury	Away
	"	30		Home
	November	6	Beverley	Home
	"	13	York	Away
	"	20	Leeds Parish Church	Home
	"	27	Whitwood	Away
	December	4	Tadcaster	Home
	"	11	Wakefield United	Away
	"	18	Doncaster	Home
	"	27	Stanley St. Peter's	Away
1887	January	1	Leeds St. John's	Home
	"	8	Hessle	Away
	"	15	Dewsbury	Home
	"	22	Leeds St. John's	Away
	"	29	Doncaster	Away
	February	5	Beverley	Away
	"	12	York	Home
	"	19	Whitwood	Home
	"	26	Tadcaster	Away
	March	5	Sheffield	Home
	"	12	South Milford	Away
	"	19	Stanley St. Peter's	Home
	"	26		Away
	April	2	Hessle	Home
	"	9	Halifax	Away
	"	11	Castleford	Away
	"	16	South Milford	Home

35

During the season over 2,600 miles were travelled to fulfil fixtures including tours to London, Cambridge and Ireland where they met defeat on a tour for the first time, against Dublin University.

Club president in 1887 was Lt. Col. Smith J.P. and Vice-Presidents were the Lord Mayor of Hull, Alderman J. S. W. Willows; the Sheriff of Hull, H. H. Briggs; Canon McCormick MA, DD (Vicar of Hull); W. J. Close; C. A. Brewer; G. A. Hoskins; F. Tindle. Club captain — Gilbert Harrison, vice-captain — H. Bell. 'A' team captain — W. D. Lyon. The treasurer was J. T. Bough of 77 Brunswick Avenue. Committee members — L. Whitehead, C. Simpson, J. Abercrombie, J. Wilson, A. B. Iveson, J. Spetch and Major H. B. Mottee. The club's Honorary Secretaries were Fred Mawer and Walter Roper of 15 Courtney Street, Holderness Road. Gilbert Harrison played for Yorkshire and so did Harry Simpson who was also the club's top try scorer with 12. George Jacketts kicked most goals. Venues for the club's A.G.M.'s were certainly varied — that year's was held at the Central Hall, Pryme Street.

By now there were about 40 teams playing regularly in the Hull area including Athletic, Central Star, Forge, East End, Marlborough, Kingston Rovers, Melbourne, South Myton, Stepney, St. Mary's, Three Crowns and Trinity but clubs that had disbanded, probably due to lack of interst, were St. John's, Church Institute, Newington, Albion, Volunteer Corps, Falcons, Holderness Foundry, Southcoates Rangers and Stoneferry.

There was a feeling that the rugby season was encroaching too much on the cricket season as the winter game took up seven months of the year.

George Jacketts   *Albert E. Bearpark*

It was proposed in 1888 that the club should revert back to all-black jerseys but this was defeated and the cherry and white strip survived for a short time. Gilbert Harrison's benefit brought him £31. Gate receipts in the season totalled nearly £1,900 and one item of expenditure was £25 for the use of Turkish Baths. A. Bearmark and G. Jacketts were both selected for Yorkshire and Hull's two matches against the 'Maoris' brought in gate receipts of £458. The top try scorer was W. Calvert and the most goals kicked by A. Kilburn. 34 matches were played, 17 won, 14 lost and 3 drawn. The match against the Maoris' on 23rd March ended in a draw, 1-1.

A proposed league for Yorkshire was announced. "An important meeting of the leading Yorkshire football clubs was convened last night at Wakefield, to consider the desirability of forming a football league. The Wakefield, Dewsbury, and Halifax clubs have received satisfactory information from the leagues of clubs who play the association game."

"Besides the clubs named, Manningham and Castleford have signified their intentions to join the new league; and Bradford, York, Hull and others are expected to follow. The new league will curtail the County Committee's power, and increase the gates as all matches will be cup ties and abolish professionalism."

The following were the secretary's names and addresses of clubs belonging to the Hull and District Rugby Football Union:

Three Crowns	— J. H. Jackson, 26 Hedon Road.
Southcoates	— J. S. Briggs, 25 Bright Street.
Beverley	— T. Rennard, Walkergate, Beverley.
Goole	— W. W. Belton, 14 North Street, Goole.
Hull	— H. Hildreth, 65 Brunswick Avenue.
St. Mary's	— A. Drewery, Montrose Terrace, Stanley Street.
Kingston Rovers	— G. Batty, Abercrombie Hotel, Campbell Street.
White Star	— C. H. Savage, 16 Woodhouse Street, Hedon Road.
Melbourne	— T. Egan, Lowgate.
Beverley Rising Star	— S. Loft, Potter Hill, Beverley.
Stepney	— E. Walkington, 68 Francis Street West.
Britannia	— G. Bulmer, Marlborough Terrace, Norfolk Street.
Forge	— C. H. Holdgate, 4 Witty Terrace, Gibson Street.

J. E. LITTLEFIELD, Hon. Sec. pro tem, Hull and District Rugby Union.

Hull's lease on their ground expired in 1889. The Southcoates club had become virtually a nursery club for Hull while other local junior clubs who provided players included Marlborough, Three Crowns, Stepney Athletics, Holderness Wanderers, Stoneferry and Beverley. A. Iveson and T. Brennan headed the try scorers' list and H. Thompson was "a champion goal kicker, top of the season's list". A Mr. Stuart of Waterworks Street was thanked in the annual report "for once again providing pineapples for the players." The season's playing record was fourteen wins, seventeen defeats and five draws.

Thursday, 17th April 1890.
Hull Daily Mail,

Manningham — the last club on Hull's fixture card — completely demolished what was supposed to be our first fifteen last Saturday (12th April) I say "supposed" because of all the poor teams Hull has taken away this season, Saturday's combination was the worst. This is the mixture which the seaport sent to do battle at Valley Parade:- full-back, Bearpark: three-quarter backs, P. Biglin, H. Thompson, and G. Calvert: half-backs, A. P. Iveson and Cook: forwards, Jacketts (captain), Galbraith, McWatt, Wright, W. Biglin, Drax, McDonnack, Parker, and Woodcock. Of course, they were never in it with the good team Manningham put in the field, and suffered defeat to the extent of 4 goals, 2 tries, and 2 minors to 2 minors (14-0). A nice thing this is for the end of the season. I think I have already wasted too much space, and will here drop my pen.

At the club's annual meeting, a resolution was passed not to enter any team in local cup competitions.

The Hull Corporation Property Committee held a meeting in the Town Hall on Friday 5th December, with Alderman Leak presiding when Hull requested the use of the Corn Exchange in High Street for practice. It was proposed by Mr. Gillet, seconded by Mr. G. Hall, to grant the application subject to the club agreeing to make good any damage and to pay for gas consumed.

The members of the club held a meeting at the Queen's Hotel and it was decided to discard the cherry and white stripes and substitute black jerseys with the borough coat of arms on the left breast, white knickerbockers and black stockings.

FIRST TEAM

Date			Club	Ground
1890	September	6	Opening Match	Home
	"	13	Halifax	Home
	"	20	Widnes	Away
	"	27	Otley	Home
	October	4	Leeds Parish Church	Home
	"	11	Huddersfield	Home
	"	13	T. R. Sutton's Team	Home
	"	18	Manningham	Away
	"	25	Halifax	Away
	November	1	Hartlepool Rovers	Home
	"	8	Brighouse Rangers	Away
	"	15	Holbeck	Home
	"	22	Otley	Away
	"	29	Leeds Parish Church	Away
	December	6	Leeds	Home
	"	13	Hunslet	Away
	"	20	Hartlepool Rovers	Away

FIRST TEAM

Date			Club	Ground
1890	December	26	Widnes	Home
	"	27	Holbeck	Away
	January	3	Rochdale Hornets	Home
	"	10	Cardiff Harlequins	Home
	"	17	Brighouse Rangers	Home
	"	24	Castleford	Away
	"	31	York	Away
	February	7	Llanelly) _ (Welsh	Away
	"	9	Cardiff Harl.) (Tour	Away
1891	"	14	Hunslet	Home
	"	21	Huddersfield	Away
	"	28	Leeds	Away
	March	7	Tad'ster or Dudley Hill	Away
	"	14		Home
	"	21	Rochdale Hornets	Away
	"	28	York	Away
	"	30	Castleford	Home
	April	4	Manningham	Home

"A" TEAM

Date			Club	Ground
1890	September	6	Opening Match	Home
	"	13	Sowerby Bridge	Away
	"	20	Beverley	Home
	"	27		Away
	October	4	Leeds Parish Church	Away
	"	11	Tadcaster	Away
	"	13	Hull Fair Day Match	Home
	"	18	Manningham	Home
	"	25	Sowerby Bridge	Home
	November	1		Away
	"	8	Brighouse Rangers	Home
	"	15	Holbeck	Away
	"	22	Normanton St. John's	Home
	"	29	Leeds Parish Church	Home
	December	6	Leeds	Away
	"	18	Hunslet	Home
	"	20		Home
	"	26	Beverley	Away
	"	27	Holbeck	Home
1891	January	3	Hebden Bridge	Away
	"	10		Away
	"	17	Brighouse Rangers	Away

"A" TEAM

Date			Club	Ground
1891	January	24	Castleford	Home
	"	31	York	Away
	February	7		Home
	"	14	Hunslet	Away
	"	21		Home
	"	28	Leeds	Home
	March	7	Tadcaster	Home
	"	14		Away
	"	21		Home
	"	28	York	Home
	"	30	Castleford	Away
	April	4	Manningham	Away
	"	11	Hebden Bridge	Home
	"	18	Normanton St. John's	Away

The club's Headquarters in 1890 were at the Queen's Hotel in Charlotte Street where William Teal was proprietor. Wm. F. B. Calvert was 'mine host' at the Plimsoll Hotel in Witham, George Hoskins had a plumbing and gasfitting business in Wilton Terrace and Church Lane, and Fred Mawer ran a sports outfitting business in Witham. The club's official colours were changed back to all-black. During the season, 65,556 adults and 6,330 juniors paid for admission.

Thirty-four matches were played and fifteen were won, sixteen lost and three drawn. Top try scorer was J. W. Anderson and J. Sparviere kicked the most goals. William Herbert Wiles was signed from local club Marlborough, where he had been club captain. He commenced his playing career with St. Georges at the age of 14.

Gilbert Harrison was Club President in 1891, when a loss of £145.1s.8d. was announced. Thirty-five matches were played and fifteen were won, seventeen lost and three drawn.

FIRST TEAM

Date			Club	Ground
1891	September	19	Opening Match	Home
	"	26	Huddersfield	Home
	October	3	Holbeck	Home
	"	10	Batley	Home
	"	12	Manningham	Home
	"	17	Leeds Parish Church	Away
	"	24	Rochdale Hornets	Away
	"	31	Otley	Away
	November	7	Brighouse Rangers	Home
	"	14	Hunslet	Away

FIRST TEAM

Date			Club	Ground
1891	November	21	Otley	Home
	"	28	Leeds Parish Church	Home
	December	5	Heckmondwike	Away
	"	12	Hunslet	Home
	"	19	Hartlepool Rovers	Away
	"	26	Liversedge Old	Home
1892	January	2	Heckmondwike	Home
	"	9	Holbeck	Away
	"	16	Leeds	Away
	"	23	Castleford	Home
	"	30	York	Away
	February	6	Brighouse Rangers	Away
	"	13	Southern Tour	Away
	"	20	Hartlepool Rovers	Home
	"	27	Batley	Away
	March	1	Halifax	Home
	"	5	Leeds	Home
	"	12	Liversedge Old	Away
	"	19	Y.C.C.T. Morley	Home
	"	26		Away
	April	2	Huddersfield	Away
	"	9	York	Home
	"	16	Castleford	Away
	"	18	Rochdale Hornets	Home
	"	19	Halifax	Away
	"	23	Manningham	Away

"A" TEAM

Date			Club	Ground
1891	September	19	Opening Match	Home
	"	26	Beverley	Away
	October	3	Holbeck	Away
	"	10	Batley	Away
	"	12	Manningham	Away
	"	17	Leeds Parish Church	Home
	"	24	York Garrison	Home
	"	31		Home
	November	7	Brighouse Rangers	Away
	"	14	Hunslet	Home
	"	21		Away
	"	28	Leeds Parish Church	Away
	December	5	Rothwell	Home
	"	12	Hunslet	Away
	"	19		Home

"A" TEAM

Date			Club	Ground
1891	December	26	Liversedge Old	Away
1892	January	2	Rothwell	Away
	"	9	Holbeck	Home
	"	16	Leeds	Home
	"	23	Castleford	Away
	"	30	York	Home
	February	6	Brighouse Rangers	Home
	"	13	York Leeman Wand'rs	Home
	"	20	York Garrison	Away
	"	27	Batley	Home
	March	5	Leeds	Away
	"	12	Liversedge Old	Home
	"	19		Away
	"	26		Home
	April	2	Beverley	Home
	"	9	York	Away
	"	16	Castleford	Home
	"	18	York Leeman Wand'rs	Home
	"	23	Manningham	Home

Patrons of the club included Evans Fraser, F.R.C.S.; F. B. Grotarian, M.P.; H. S. King, M.P.; C. H. Wilson, M.P. and Sir A. K. Rollit, M.P. New dressing rooms were built at the ground and J. Mather of 136 Wincolmlee advertised himself as "official sole contractor for boots for Hull F.C." A. Shillito with seven tries was top of the scores list and J. Sparviere topped the goal kickers list for the second successive season.

Monday, 18th April 1892.
Hull Daily Mail,

DISTURBANCE ON THE FOOTBALL FIELD

After the match Hull 'A' v Castleford 'A', a remarkable scene took place. Two of the Castleford men set on Hardacker. An old player, named Friston, in supporting him, was laid low. It was also stated among the crowd that one of the visitors had kicked the referee. However this may have been, the mob immediately took the matter in hand, rushed on the field and assaulted the Castleford men who had been the originators of the disturbance. At the time of writing the mob had imprisoned Castleford, who were confined to the dressing-room on the field.

FIRST TEAM

Date			Club	Ground
1892	September	8	Leeds	Away
	"	10	York	Home
	"	17	Liversedge	Away
	"	24	Brighouse Rangers	Away

FIRST TEAM

Date			Club	Ground
1892	October	1	Leeds Parish Church	Home
	"	8	Batley	Away
	"	10	Manningham	Home
	"	15	Otley	Home
	"	22	Hartlepool Rovers	Home
	"	29	Holbeck	Away
	November	5	Hunslet	Home
	"	12		
	"	19	York	Away
	"	26	Brighouse Rangers	Home
	December	3	Bramley	Away
	"	10	Batley	Home
	"	17	Pontefract	Away
	"	24	Leeds Parish Church	Away
	"	26	Pontefract	Home
	"	31		
1893	January	7	Manningham	Away
	"	14		
	"	21		
	"	28	Holbeck	Home
	February	4	Leeds	Home
	"	11		Home
	"	18	Heckmondwike (Charity)	Home
	"	25	Otley	Away
	March	4	Heckmondwike	Away
	"	11	Hunslet	Away
	"	18	Y.C.C.T. Leeds	Home
	"	25	"	Away
	April	1		
	"	3	Halifax	Away
	"	8	Hartlepool Rovers	Away
	"	15	Halifax	Home
	"	22	Bramley	Home
	"	29	Liversedge	Home

"A" TEAM

Date			Club	Ground
1892	September	3	Leeds	Home
	"	10	York	Away
	"	17	Liversedge	Home
	"	24	Brighouse Rangers	Home
	October	1	Leeds Parish Church	Away
	"	8	Batley	Home
	"	10		
	"	15		
	"	22		
	"	29	Holbeck	Home
	November	5	Hunslet	Away
	"	12		
	"	19	York	Home
	"	26	Brighouse Rangers	Away
	December	3	Bramley	Home
	"	10	Batley	Away
	"	17	Pontefract	Home
	"	24	Leeds Parish Church	Home
	"	26	Pontefract	Away
	"	31		
1893	January	7		
	"	14		
	"	21		
	"	28	Holbeck	Away
	February	4	Leeds	Away
	"	11		
	"	18	Halifax Crescent	Away
	"	25		
	March	4	Halifax Crescent	Home
	"	11	Hunslet	Home
	"	18		
	"	25	Luddendenfoot	Away
	April	1		
	"	3	Luddendenfoot	Home
	"	8		
	"	15		
	"	22	Bramley	Away
	"	29	Liversedge	Away

The President of the club in 1892 was W. J. Close and the club captain was L. Donkin. The Mona Club from the Isle of Man were hosted and the Club's directors signed a renewal lease on the ground, thereby squashing strong rumours of a move to new headquarters. The season's playing record was 20 wins, 14 defeats and 3 draws.

Wednesday, 8th February 1893:

HULL 7   v.   HECKMONDWIKE 7

Hull	Heckmondwike
Walt Mansell	Knowles
W. Johnson	Oates
C. Jefferies — 1 Goal	Ellis
J. Timson	Jones — 1 Try
C. H. Tullock	Clough
A. Larard — 1 Try	G. Harrison
A. McKay — 1 Try	Jowett — 1 Try : 1 Goal
L. Donkin	S. Harrison
A. C. Bearpark	Walford
J. Holmes	Harland
H. G. Waters	Robertson
R. Roberts	Halliday
T. Marsden	Ackroyd
F. Harrison	Welsh
C. Rhodes	(only 14 played)

Half-time 2—2   Attendance 8,000

This game was played under "Electric Light" — without doubt Hull's first ever floodlit game. The *Hull Daily Mail* account stated that 8 arc lamps each of 1,000 candle power were set up and the generator for the lamps was powered by a Priestman Oil Engine situated under the West Stand. "The spectators in the East and West stands were able to obtain a good view".

Hull were drafted into the Yorkshire Senior Competition in 1893 but finished a disappointing 10th out of 12 clubs. Fred Mawer resigned as Club Secretary and G. W. Stephenson joined Hy. Hildreth as joint Hon. Secretary. The Hull Gymnastic Society offered the rugby club the use of their facilities for training purposes, an offer which was gratefully accepted. The services of the local police cost £14 during the season. Over 95,000 paid for admission at home matches. Will Mansell was top try scorer with six. Clubs made representation to the Rugby Football Union in September that players be compensated for loss of earnings (broken time) as the working week then was 6 days. The motion was lost by 282 votes to 136.

Friday, 22nd September 1893.
Hull Daily Mail,

YORKSHIRE RUGBY UNION

The Pall Mall Gazette says:- Yorkshire received a severe snubbing last night at the meeting of the Rugby Union in the rejection of its plan for the introduction of professionalism. The proposal to compensate players for loss of time, brought forward by Mr. Miller, was defeated by an enormous majority, more than two to one; and it is safe to say that we have heard the last of it for some time. There is practically no grievance in the present state of affairs, and we are astonished that Yorkshire and Lancashire should think there is. The southerner does not grumble and pull long faces because in order to play a match he has to sacrifice half a day or more. If the game is worth playing, it is worth playing for its own sake, and worth playing at some cost. Of course, if it could be shown that the existence of professionals would go to improve the technical skills of football, as it is the case with cricket, that would be quite another matter, but no one would advance such an argument.

FIRST TEAM

Date			Club	Ground
1893	September	2	Rochdale Hornets	Away
	"	9	*Liversedge Old	Home
	"	16	*Leeds	Home
	"	23	*Halifax	Away
	"	30	*Huddersfield	Home
	October	7	Leeds Parish Church	Away
	"	11	Heckmondwike	Home
	"	14	*Batley	Home
	"	21	*Wakefield Trinity	Away
	"	28	*Manningham	Home
	November	4	*Brighouse Rangers	Away
	"	11	*Wakefield Trinity	Home
	"	18	*Bradford	Away
	"	25	*Brighouse Rangers	Home
	December	2	*Dewsbury	Home
	"	9	*Halifax	Home
	"	16	*Hunslet	Home
	"	23	*Leeds	Away
	"	26	Broughton	Home
	"	30	Otley	Home
1894	January	1	Broughton	Away
	"	6	*Huddersfield	Away
	"	13	Tour	Away
	"	20	Heckmondwike	Away
	"	27	*Bradford	Home
	February	3	*Batley	Away
	"	10	*Dewsbury	Away
	"	17	*Liversedge	Away
	"	24	*Hunslet	Away
	March	3	*Manningham	Away
	"	10		
	"	17	Cup Ties — Elland	Away
	"	23	Blackley	Home
	"	24	Cup Ties	
	"	26	Leeds Parish Church	Home
	"	31	Cup Ties	

Date			Club	Ground
1894	April	7	Rochdale Hornets	Home
	"	14	Hartlepool Rovers	Home
	"	21	Otley	Away
	"	28	Hartlepool Rovers	Away

* COMPETITION MATCHES.

37 matches were played, 19 won, 16 lost and 2 drawn.

"A" TEAM

Date			Club	Ground
1893	September	2	York Fulford Rovers	Home
	"	9	York Fulford Rovers	Away
	"	16	Leeds	Away
	"	23	Halifax	Home
	"	30	Huddersfield	Away
	October	7	Leeds Parish Church	Home
	"	11	Hull Fair Day Match	Home
	"	14	Batley	Away
	"	21	Wakefield Trinity	Home
	"	28	Manningham	Away
	November	4	Brighouse Rangers	Home
	"	11	Wakefield Trinity	Away
	"	18	Bradford	Home
	"	25	Brighouse Rangers	Away
	December	1	Dewsbury	Away
	"	9	Halifax	Away
	"	16	Hunslet	Away
	"	23	Leeds	Home
	"	26	Beverley	Away
	"	30		Away
1894	January	1	New Year Day Match	Away
	"	6	Huddersfield	Home
	"	13		Home
	"	20	Whitwood	Home
	"	27	Bradford	Away
	February	3	Batley	Home
	"	10	Dewsbury	Home
	"	17	Goole	Home
	"	24	Hunslet	Home
	March	3	Manningham	Home
	"	10	Whitwood	Away
	"	17		
	"	23	Good Friday Match	Home
	"	24	Beverley	Home

Date			Club	Ground
1894	March	26	Leeds Parish Church	Away
	"	31	Ripon	Away
	April	7	Garforth	Away
	"	14	Goole	Away
	"	21	Garforth	Home
	"	28	Ripon	Home

A tour of the Lake District was undertaken in 1894/5. The Trippett Baths in Wincolmlee were hired from Hull Corporation Council for £23 and used for changing and washing accommodation. The club's directors laid the basis for a momentous decision when they entered into negotiations for a ten year lease of the Athletic Grounds, near the Boulevard, at a rent of £150 a year. Their tenure of the Holderness Road ground was uncertain but after signing a lease for the Athletic Grounds, the directors changed their minds and decided to stay in the east of the city. However the directors of the Athletic Grounds held them to their contract. A scheme to lease the two grounds never really got off the ground and the Holderness Road venue was sold off for building land. Hull Kingston Rovers had been playing at the Athletic Grounds and they moved across the River Hull to a ground in Craven Street off Holderness Road.

Hull finished 11th out of 12 clubs and had the remarkable record of not scoring in 12 of their 22 league matches. Cyril C. Lempriere had the distinction of captaining the club during their last full season at Holderness Road and the first one at the Athletic Grounds. Nicknamed 'Lemp', he was a wing-threequarter and made his club debut in 1892, scoring 5 tries in 26 matches. He began playing rugby with Radley College in 1886 and then played with Worcester College, Oxford, between 1889 and 1892 and occasionally turned out for Oxford University. At this time Gilbert Harrison died. Born at Cottingham, he was an early stalwart of the club. Off the field he was a partner in Harrison Brothers, corn merchants, in High Street. £25 was donated to wives and children suffering through the Hull dock strike, as many of the club's fans worked on the docks.

It was a time of real change for club and country — a new government, ground location and constitution.

38 matches were played, 13 won, 22 lost and 3 drawn.

C. C. Lempriere.

48

THE HULL CLUB'S TOUR

Descriptive Account by the *Hull Times* special "Full Back"

I concluded my first article, which was confined to a description of the journey from Hull to Plymouth with the expression that my first night's rest at the Globe Hotel would be undisturbed. But, alas! my hopes were doomed to bitter disappointment. Instead of the long railway journey inducing sleep it had entirely the opposite effect, for a more active lot than the Hull team — about one o'clock on Saturday morning last — I have never had as companions. For fully two hours the corridors and bedrooms were the scenes of suppressed, but, nevertheless, hearty fun. Players were hoisted out of their rooms, beds were disarranged, and until three o'clock there was nothing but

A SILENT PANDEMONIUM

"Billy" Mansell was perhaps the quietest of the lot. There was no need to tell him that "his number was up, and he would have to go." Oh, dear no. It's impossible for him to lay himself open to justify such an order. Eventually nature asserted herself, and all fell into a deep sleep before the clock chimed half past three. Jack Chaffer and Jack Holmes were the first pair to shake off sleep and they roamed the corridors on the look out. A pair of boots were outside one of the rooms, and in the twinkle of an eye Chaffer had filled both with water, whilst Holmes shook with laughter and encouraged his companion in the mischievous act. But his face was a study when he suddenly discovered the boots were his own, and the penalty he paid for his share in the transaction was a couple of hours confinement in the hotel. An early call and then the players were conducted to the Devonport Dockyard — a spacious and wonderful place. The points of interest were clearly explained by a dockworker, who acted as a guide, and every interesting sight was met with the observation

"VERY GOOD IDEA".

The ironclads and old fashioned battle-ships lying side by side formed a striking comparison between the ancient and the modern mode of warfare, the work shops, and stupendous warehouses filled us with admiration, and the visit to the yard was thoroughly enjoyed. One circumstance was very noticeable, viz, the presence of a large amount of superfluous labour, which led the factious Dannatt to suggest that the following notice would be very appropriate:- "Any employees found sweating in this establishment will be instantly dismissed." A return was made to Plymouth on the trains, and after lunch the Hull players dressed for the match with Devonport Albion, the crack team of the west of England. Other players had arrived in the town after travelling all night and the full party from Hull consisted of Messrs. W. Close (president), Clubley, H. Dannatt, Donkin, Chaffer, Jacketts, Wiles, "Billy" Mansell, Alf Mennell, Charlie Hunter, Bob Wray, W. Johnson, Jeffreys, Duncan Wright, Jack Holmes, Billy Wright, Herb Thompson, Denton, Brinham, McLachlan, "Clogger" Fletcher, Tommy Allen, Jacques, Jim Grey, and

MYSELF.

The Players arrived at the ground, some considerable distance away, in pretty good time. There was a crowd of 5,000 to 6,000; but the important

Association match between Devon and Cornwall in the neighbourhood attracted a large number who would otherwise be present. A grand game was witnessed, and, as everybody knows, the "tourists" won by eight points to six. Mansell's drop goal was a piece of sharp work, and as for Jeffery's — well, I never saw a prettier in my life. Hull's victory was very popular, especially amongst the sailors and soldiers — many of them hail from Yorkshire — and the enthusiasm which prevailed as the Hull team, full of spirits, were driving from the field I will never forget. Without exaggeration, thousands lined the footpath and hedges, and the cheering, as the players drove through the human avenue, was something to be remembered. One of the Plymouth papers — the *Western Daily Mercury* — in commenting on the match, passed some very severe strictures on Hull's play, evidently written by a man who knew

VERY LITTLE OF THE GAME.

The Albion team did occasionally play rough but on the whole the match was a splendid exhibition, and the encouraging shouts of "Up Hull" and the favourable criticism of the *Western Morning News* gives a contradiction of the paper in question. In the evening the majority of the team visited the Grand Theatre, and an allusion by "Mother Goose" to Hull's victory was appreciated in hearty Yorkshire fashion. All hands assembled — oh, yes, every one — at the Globe shortly after eleven o'clock and on the principle "early to bed early to rise" the party were in the upper regions in decent time. But not to rest. That was out of the question — at least for an hour or two. There was a mimic warfare in which bolsters, pillows, boots, and bed-clothing played a prominent part. An hour or so of this sort of fun sufficed, and all the team — even Chaffer, Mansell, Mennell, Thompson, and Fletcher — found refuge in bed. On Sunday an early breakfast was provided, and then a visit was payed to the famous Plymouth Hoe, the Broadwater, and the Fortress. The parade of soldiers belonging to the various denominations before their march to chapel or church was also witnessed, and returned to the Globe Hotel.

A COUPLE OF DRAGS

were in waiting to convey the party to Dousdale, a small village about 14 miles away, and four miles distance from the Convict Prison. Chaffer and Wiles were compelled to return by the one o'clock train, reaching Hull at five the next morning, were unable to take part in the excursion, and they parted sadly from their comrades at the hotel door with looks of envy on their faces. At Dousdale an excellent dinner was served, and an opportunity for rest and a quiet smoke was afforded in a comfortable room. The country was lovely, and in picturesque character has to be seen to be believed, but I am forbidden into entering into an elaborate description of the outing, simply because I have no space at my disposal. As the bells were

CHIMING FOR CHURCH

the conveyance returned to Plymouth. In the evening nearly all the players visited the sacred concert on the Pier and the music of the band, the singing, and the promenade was a pleasant change. This was the last night of the team's stay in Plymouth, and as a natural consequence the members were not particular how they enjoyed themselves, so long as they did so. Shortly after closing hours the party had returned to their headquarters, and preparations were made for what the "jovial crew" termed "receptions". First of all one or two of the bolder spirits put all the bedrooms in a state of "topsy turveyism", and the prospect of a quiet night's rest was indeed remote. The more fortunate ones placed themselves out of the reach of harm by drawing chests of drawers and bedsteads up to the room doors, the barricades offering an effectual resistance to the strongest attacks. Those who had not taken this necessary precaution suffered.

Jackett's reception was a pronounced success, and for a considerable time fun ran riot. Mr. Jacques, M. S. and L. — miserable, slow and lazy I am told the affixes stand for — was the essence of mischief, and Mansell, Thompson, "Billy" Wright, Jack Holmes, Jefferys, Johnson, Fletcher, Tommy Allen, and last but by no means least, Harry Dannatt entered into the spirit of enjoyment with enthusiasm. The quiet ones consisted of Donkin, Denton (my bedmate), Jacketts, Duncan Wright, Gray, McLachlan, Brinham, Bob Wray, and myself, all of whom with beating hearts, were waiting for the turbulent crowd to relapse into silence. It was not until their tormenting resources failed they sought their beds, and they were beds, too. There was nothing but the frames standing, the clothing having been flung anywhere, and only those whose dramatic experiences have enabled them to acquire the art of bed making obtained sleep in reasonable(?) time. In the morning the team departed for Exeter, and so pleasant and enjoyable had the landlord of the Globe found the stay of his guests that

BIG SALT TEARS

coursed down his cheeks as from the steps he bade them "Bon Voyage". Exeter was reached at 12 o'clock, and in the afternoon the strongest team Exeter could place in the field went down to the Hull fifteen in a drouching rain. After the match, Messrs. Close, Cubley, Donkin, Denton, and Hunter travelled home by the evening train, and the remainder — "their numbers were up, and they had to go" followed in the saloon on Tuesday, reaching Hull at seven o'clock. The journey home was pleasantly passed, singing, joking, and other forms of entertainment, together with a capital lunch making the time fly all too quickly. The tour was the best ever arranged by the Hull Club, and the amusing incidents which occurred during the five days' absence of the team would

FILL A VOLUME.

The night and day fun was rampant, and there was not a single circumstance to mar the success of the tour. The weather was summer like —with the exception of the rain at Exeter — there was every opportunity of entertainment, the scenery was magnificent, and the team were "fed" — if I must use a vulgar word, in the absence of a better — in a manner which makes my mouth water whenever my thoughts carry me back. Jefferys suggested that the Hull F.C. committee should send the team down to Plymouth during the summer to prepare them for the next season. If they do there will be no need for Bob Wray to shout "anyone ill?" — by the way, a famous rallying cry during the tour —for they would come back full of vigour and freshness, notwithstanding that Plymouth is said to be an unhealthy town. On Tuesday there was only one regret — a regret in which I shared — and that was that the tour had come to a termination.

51

But all things have an end, and all there is now to look forward to is a series of stern fights to uphold the prestige of the club. May the team come forth in resplendent glory clothed with the mantle of victory is my sincere wish. Messrs. Close, Cubley, and Dannatt have had a great deal of responsibility resting upon their shoulders, but they have emerged from the ordeal well, and are entitled to the fullest measure of praise for the able manner in which they handled the arrangements.

Saturday, 29th September 1894.
The Hull Times,

THE HULL FOOTBALL CLUB'S GROUND

Hull News, 7th September:- "The Hull Football Club have, so we are informed, entered into a 10 year agreement with the Athletic Ground Company Limited, to occupy their capitally appointed ground."

Hull Times, 8th September:- "The negotiations re the ground had been left in the hands of a sub-committee, and so far nothing definite has been decided on."

Hull News, 11th September:- "The miserable manner in which the statement that the Hull F. C. had taken the Athletic Ground on a ten year lease.... was contradicted by a contemporary on Saturday evening does not say much for the veracity of the artist who penned the denial in that cocksure style.... The statement that the Hull Football Club have come to terms with the Hull Athletics Ground Company to lease their ground for ten years is perfectly correct."

Daily Mail, 17th September:- "That an agreement has been entered into is absolutely false, and has no foundation in fact.... At a meeting of the Athletic Ground Company last Friday night two applications came before the directors — one from Hull and the other from Kingston Rovers. No decision was arrived at."

Hull News, 18th September:- "As I said last week, respecting the Hull Football Club, almost everything has been settled for a general flit next season from the Holderness Road ground to the Athletic Ground.... Again we must express our sincere apologies to our contemporary for having been first to announce the important fact. Next please."

Hull News, 25th September:- "The Athletic Company's ground is still to be knocked down to the highest bidder. Who is it to be? Hull or Rovers?"

Saturday, 27th October.
The Hull Times,

HULL FOOTBALL CLUB AND THE ATHLETIC GROUND
MEETING OF MEMBERS

A specially convened meeting of members of the Hull Football Club was held at the Gladstone Hall, Albion Street, last night to take into consideration the proposed scheme for taking over the Athletic Ground, Boulevard. Mr. C. Brewer (president) occupied the chair, and amongst those present were:- Mr. W. C. Townsend (hon. solicitor), Messrs. W. J. Close, L. Cubley, F. Tindle, and L. Whitehead (vice-presidents), A. Mennell, ('A' team captain), A. Bird (hon. Treasurer), J. A. Adams, F. Bowes, J. H. Dannatt, G. A. Hoskins,

G. Jacketts, W. D. Lyon, and J. W. Porter (committee), and H. Hildreth and G. W. Stephenson (hon. secretaries). The Chairman having briefly stated the object of the meeting, gave way to Mr. W. C. Townsend, who detailed the scheme. He explained the agreement, the draft of which has been published, and also been forwarded to the members of the club. He pointed out that according to the rules the committee were not obliged to bring the matter before the whole body of members, but they felt it their duty to do so.

TEST THE FEELING OF ALL.

The Chairman moved, "That this meeting of the Hull Football Club, having explained to them the terms and conditions of the provisional agreement, 20th October, 1894, made between the Hull Athletic Ground Company on the other part and Mr. Charles Albert Brewer for and on behalf of this club on the other part, hereby expresses its approval of the same, and authorises the president and committee to carry the same into effect, conditionally that before the lease is signed a scheme shall be prepared by the committee converting the club into a limited company, which scheme shall contain proper provisions for

DIVIDING BY WAY OF SHARES

in such company the present funds of the club amongst its members equally." He stated that if the resolution was carried they would have an assured tenancy. To the Executive Committee it had always been a matter of anxiety that they had such an insecure tenancy. It had always stulified them in their actions. If they decided to change they would have a lease to protect them for 10 years if nothing further was done. Financially it would effect a great saving. The more they went into details the more they would be convinced that it would be a great benefit to the club to accept the terms. This was seconded by Mr. W. J. Close. Answering Mr. Bough, Mr. Townsend said they proposed by the conversion to take away from each individual member the responsibility of a single farthing, and divide the funds of the club amongst the members. As to whether shareholders in the Athletic Company could vote on the question there was no law to prevent them and the matter must be

LEFT TO THEIR CONSCIENCE.

The Holderness Road ground had not been sold, but they could take it from him that the club would not have the front part of the ground. Mr. Hoskins: Has the club received notice to remove from the Holderness Road? Mr. Townsend: No they have not. Replying to Mr. Yull, the Chairman said if they took the ground, arrangements would be made for bringing the spectators as near to the field of play as at present. Mr. Ayre moved the previous question which Mr. Yull seconded. On being put to the vote the motion was defeated. A division was demanded: 69 voted for Mr. Ayre's motion and 102 against. A proposition that the meeting should be adjourned was not entertained. Eventually, after further discussion, the original resolution was passed.

Saturday. 4th May 1895.
The Hull Times,

WILL THEY LEAVE HOLDERNESS ROAD?

It will be remembered that on terminating their lease with the proprietors of the Holderness Road ground, the Hull Football Club concluded an arrangement with the Hull Athletic Ground Company to take over the Boulevard enclosure, which was last occupied by Kingston Rovers, for ten years at £150 per annum. Within the past few days there has been the prospect —now exceedingly remote — of continuing the tenancy of the Holderness Road ground. Originally the owners of the field upon which Hull has played for so many years contemplated making two streets, running parallel from Holderness Road and they offered the Hull Football Club the large field used by the B team at 2s 6d a yard. It was felt by Hull that the cost of placing the ground in a suitable condition and the renewal of the field of play from the main thoroughfare would be prejudicial to their interests. They thereupon opened negotiations with the Athletic Ground Company, and subsequently an agreement was signed. Just recently, however, Messrs. Rolitt and Sons, who have acted for the owners of the Holderness Road property, came forward with an offer to sell the entire land — the first and the B team ground — at 1s 6d a yard. Of course, the change to become the possessors on such reasonable terms was appreciated by the Hull committee, and an effort was made to

REVOKE MUTUALLY THE AGREEMENT

entered into by the two parties. Mr. W. C. Townsend, the solicitor to the Hull Football Club, communicatd with Mr. Frank Hall, secretary of the Athletic Ground Company, who brought the matter officially before his directors. The Chairman (Councillor Robson J.P.) had also had the question brought under his notice, but it was resolved, after a long discussion, not to release the club from its legal responsibilities. The directors of the Ground Company considered that it was "babyish" on the part of the Hull Football Club to enter into a serious agreement and then endeavour to revoke it within such a short time. It was mentioned by somebody at the meeting that the Football Club was prepared to give £500, if the company would agree to set aside the agreement, but nothing but its absolute fulfilment would satisfy the board. There has been a rumour in the town that Kingston Rovers were prepared to step into the gap, and undertake the responsibilities which Hull have incurred. The Hull Football Club have power to sub-let, but it is feared that matters have gone too far to permit of this step being taken. There is no question that if it could be arranged for the two principal clubs in Hull to remain on the grounds they have formerly occupied the advantage would be mutual, the only point is "could Rovers afford the high rent which the Hull Club has arranged to give?" Whatever steps are taken will have to be immediately commenced, because within a day or two the Hull Football Club will

ADVERTISE THE SALE OF THEIR STANDS

and other effects on the Holderness Road. A stringent condition of sale will be that the property bought must be removed from the ground within seven days of purchase, so therefore it would not be open to a football club to enter into competition. In enforcing this condition, the action of the Hull Committee is obvious. Perhaps before the Holderness Road ground is converted into building land pure and simple, and for ever destroyed as a football enclosure, some of the Rovers' supporters will come to the front in a manner which will enable the consistent Hessle Road contingent to enter upon a fresh lease of life. In the event of nothing happening which will interrupt the existing arrangement, the Hull Football Club will take possession of the Athletic Ground for 10 years, but Rovers' fate has yet to be determined. A portable stand in 15 or 20 sections, will be placed across the green at the Hessle Road end of the field. It will be so constructed that in the summer time it can be removed without difficulty, and in the matter of accommodation 1,400 people will be provided for. It is suggested that the present grand-stand should be lengthened and that on the Division Road side, or immediately opposite, another stand, 75 yards long, should be built. We do not believe it is intended to make any alterations at the Anlaby Road end of an important character, but in all probability, improvements will be effected in the dressing rooms. On four principal grounds in Yorkshire — Headingley, Huddersfield, Halifax, and Bradford — there are telegraph offices, and all but Bradford have built entensive refreshment rooms, which are a source of profit. The Hull Committee might consider the advisability of doing the same, with the advantage to themselves and the public generally.

Chapter Five
THE BIG SPLIT

Saturday, 11th May 1895.
The Hull Times,

RUGBY UNION

THE LANCASHIRE-YORKSHIRE SCHEME CONDEMNED

Last night we received the resolutions which were passed by the Rugby Union Committee at their meeting held on Thursday at the Craven Hotel, Charing Cross, London.

They are as follows:-

"This committee, being of the opinion that any such organisation as the proposed union of Lancashire and Yorkshire clubs would be prejudicial to the best interests of the game, forbids the formation of such a union."

Saturday, 31st August 1895.
The Hull Times,

THE RUGBY SPLIT.

NORTHERN UNION FORMED

At the George Hotel, Huddersfield, on Thursday night, one of the principal Rugby football clubs in the North of England took the final steps of deciding the dispute with the authorities, and their representatives forwarded to Mr. G. Rowland Hill, the hon. secretary of the English Rugby Football Union, the resignation from that body. All the senior Yorkshire clubs were represented, and nine of the leading Lancashire clubs. The proceedings were private, but at the conclusion of the meeting it was stated that Mr. Waller and Mr. Platt had requested to act as president and secretary *pro tem* of the organisation respectively. After full discussion the following resolution had been adopted:-

"That the clubs here represented decide to form a Northern Rugby Football Union, and pledge themselves to push forward, without delay, its establishment on the principle of payment for *bona fide* broken time only. It was agreed that during the coming season there shall be Senior competitions in progress both in Lancashire and Yorkshire. Each of the constituent clubs will in the course of the season play home and away matches with each other, and the results of these engagements will count in deciding the result of the competition in which the whole of the clubs will take part for the championship of Lancashire and Yorkshire. The representatives of the whole of the twelve Yorkshire clubs who have taken part in the movement, with the exception of Dewsbury and of the whole of the nine Lancashire clubs handed to Mr. Platt their resignations from the English Rugby Union. In the case of the Dewsbury Club, Mr. Holdsworth stated that he had not yet had an opportunity of consulting his committee on the subject, and though he had no doubt that they would entirely agree with the action of the other clubs he could not accept the responsibility of forwarding the resignation. With regard to the length of the football season, it was pointed out that each of the clubs would now have to play 42 matches in the course of the season, and a resolution was passed reverting to the old system in operation in the English Rugby Union prior to this season, namely, that it should extend from 1st September to 30th April. In order that the necessary arrangements may be made as soon as possible it was decided that a meeting of the secretaries of the whole of the constituent clubs should be held on Tuesday evening next at the Spread Eagle Hotel, Manchester, at five o'clock to arrange fixtures. This will mean a complete change in present club arrangements. It was also mentioned that it had been arranged that the meetings of the new body should be held alternately in Manchester and Huddersfield.

RESIGNATION OF THE COUNTY SECRETARY.

Mr. W. Hirst, of Huddersfield, secretary of the Yorkshire Rugby Union, has decided to send in his resignation to the Yorkshire County Committee, and also to the English Rugby Union. Mr. H. H. Waller, representative of the Spen Valley district, has acted similarly.

NO PROFESSIONALISM.

A justification of the action of the Huddersfield Club in joining the new Union has been furnished by Mr. H. Beardsall, one of the club's hon. secs., to a correspondent. He says: "The decision of the committee of the club to join the Northern Union was come to after due deliberation, and they disclaim any idea of going in for professionalism, and the only question which can come prior to the ban of the English Rugby Union is that of payment for broken time, which was strongly advocated by the whole of the Yorkshire clubs two years ago."

Saturday, 31st August 1895
The Hull News,

THE FOOTBALL CRISIS

FORMATION OF THE NORTHERN RUGBY UNION

A meeting of the Yorkshire Senior clubs was held on Tuesday, at the Mitre Hotel, Leeds, to discuss the formation of the Northern Union, and the result is that the dispute which has led to the proposal has culminated in a final severance of the disaffected clubs of the two counties from the existing football authorities. The Bradford, Huddersfield, and Leeds Clubs were understood to have been adverse to the suggested union, but the pressure brought to bear upon their committees appears to have been too great, and as a matter of self-preservation they decided to be represented at the meeting and throw in their lot with the rest of the clubs concerned. Representatives of all the clubs in the late Senior Competition were accordingly present, the names being as follows

57

Mr. H. H. Waller (Brighouse), in the chair; Mr. J. Goodall (Batley), Mr. T. A. Corry (Bradford), Mr. A. Fattorini (Manningham), Mr. J. Clifford (Huddersfield), Mr. J. L. Whitaker (Hunslet), Mr. C. A. Brewer (Hull), Mr. J. E. Hampshire (Liversedge), Mr. H. Sewell (Leeds), Mr. J. Nichol (Halifax), Mr. G. Steele (Wakefield), and Mr. C. Holdsworth (Dewsbury). At the close of the meeting copies of the following resolutions were handed to the Press.

"The clubs here represented forming the late Senior Competition consider that the time is now opportune to form a Northern Rugby Football Union, and will do their utmost to push forward as rapidly as possible the establishment of such a Union."

"The Yorkshire Rugby Football Union, not having seen it advisable to appoint a sub-committee, has decided to meet a deputation of the late Senior Competition, we decided to make no further application of this subject to the above Union."

The resolutions were both carried unanimously.

The *Yorkshire Post* says:- It is stated that the scope of the new Union will be widened so as to include, in addition to those of Lancashire and Yorkshire, the Senior Clubs of other counties in the north, if applications are received from any such. Between all clubs in membership of the Union the transfer law existing under the late Senior Competition will apply, and this "poaching" on each others preserves will be impossible. But the limitations will not, of course, apply to clubs outside the Northern Union, and here it is that the clubs consider they have a very strong advantage, inasmuch as they will be able to recruit their ranks without being subject to reprisals. The situation is one that will cause perhaps more uneasiness in Welsh football circles than anywhere else, seeing that it is in the Principality that the best exponents of the modern four three-quarter play are supposed to be developed. While further details of the new scheme are awaited, it may be as well to point out that the new departure has not received the sanction of the general body of members of the clubs concerned, nor is it clear that the adoption of a movement that will be designated as professionalism will be in accord with the articles of association of some of the incorporated clubs.

Monday, 2nd September 1895.
Hull Daily Mail,

THE RUGBY SPLIT

A HULL COMMENTATOR.

In spite of all the *Yorkshire Post* has been able to do in the way of throwing cold water over the scheme, the Northern Rugby Football Union is now an accomplished fact, comprising, as it does, 22 of the most powerful clubs in the North of England, and now the oracle of that paper has to console itself by parading divers dreadful pains and penalties to which the rash ones have rendered themselves liable. First of all he who dwells upon the terrible consequences which will ensue should the Football Association forbid (as they very likely will do) the Association game to be played on the 22 grounds. We should say that none of the 22 will care very much about this excepting Leeds, and they won't suffer much. As far as the Hull club are concerned, it will affect them about as much as it would Preston North End if the English Rugby Union forbade them to play Rugby. Turning, however, to the question of how the suspension of the 22 clubs and their members would affect the status of amateur runners, this is far more serious, as many prominent players (Cooper, Baily, Firth, &c.) would give up football altogether sooner than lose their amateur qualification. In the writer's opinion there need not be the slightest anxiety on the subject. In the first place, the Rugby Union have no understanding with the Amateur Athletic Association on the subject of professionalism, and a man declared by the former body to be a pro is not necessarily ineligible to compete as an amateur runner, swimmer, boxer, &c. The A.A.A. definition of an amateur is "one who has never taught, pursued, or assisted in the pursuit of athletic exercises as a means of livelihood". And so long as this law is not infringed the suspension of the seceding clubs and their players will have no more effect with the three A's than if the 22 turned round and suspended all clubs outside themselves. The *Yorkshire Post* the other day solemnly informed its readers that even lately the A.A.A. had permanently disqualified a person "for having been a professional footballer", quite forgetting, or probably not knowing, that the man named had been a paid player of an association club. A paid football player has, of course, no more right to run or swim as an amateur than a professional cricketer or boxer, but as the new Union do not intend to pay their men anything beyond what they are actually out of pocket, there is little fear that their players will endanger their status with such a broad-minded and skilfully managed body as the Amateur Athletic Association, — JOHN S. LEEMING, HULL.

Football whether played under Association or Rugby rules was the game of the working classes in the North of England. The Football and Cricket International C. B. Fry thought it "a grand game but really more suitable for boys than men. A footballer is at his best between 20 and 25 years of age."

Except in a few large towns, Rugby and Association did not thrive well side by side. C. B. Fry thought it easier to become a moderate Rugby player than it was to attain fair skill at Association. Payment of players was illegal under the Association rules but with clubs charging entrance money, players wanted some advantage from this. There was a great struggle but professionalism was eventually legalised.

The class system influenced opinion in London and the Southern Counties against professionalism in both Association and Rugby. C. B. Fry wrote "professionalism has to a large extent split Association football as a recreation". An experimental game between Batley and Halifax with 6 forwards in teams of 13, abolished the line-out and a round ball brought Fry's report "the ball, as it deserved to, burst. A movement which is, to say the least, not quite candid, will fail of success and the seceders will speedily pass out of football history. Association football has become a game at which no gentleman can play". The establishment had to give way when Association became popular throughout the country but class distinction has remained against the predominantly Northern game of rugby league.

Chapter Six
A CHANGE OF DIRECTION

Hull severed membership with the Yorkshire and the England Rugby Unions and entered the Northern Rugby Union as founder members together with Manningham, Halifax, Runcorn, Oldham, Brighouse Rangers, Tyldesley, Hunslet, Leigh, Wigan, Bradford, Leeds, Rochdale Hornets, Warrington, St. Helens, Liversedge, Widnes, Stockport, Batley, Wakefield Trinity, Huddersfield and Broughton Rangers. After the inaugural meeting at the George Hotel, Huddersfield on 29th August, 1895, Hull's directors were empowered to pay playing members for *bona fide* broken time, i.e. payment could be made for players having to take unpaid time off work to play rugby. £195 was paid by the club for 'broken time' during the season (the agreed rate was 6/- (30p) per player per match). Gates increased and a record crowd of 15,000 watched the home match against Bradford on Good Friday.

Their first match to be played in the Northern Union was away to Batley on 7th September, when Hull went down 3-7, Holmes scoring the try. The team was: Johnson, Lempriere, Jacques, J. Townend, Duncan Wright, C. Townend, G. Baker, Mansell, Booth, Feetham, Holmes, Harmer, Carr, F. Spenceley, G. Jacketts.

First team to play for Hull at The Boulevard v Liversedge, September 21st, 1895.
Back Row: H. Hildreth (Hon. Joint Sec.), C. A. Brewer (President), G. Jacketts,
G. W. Stephenson (Hon. Joint Sec.)
Third Row: H. Wiles, W. Mansell, W. Harmer, J. S. Barker, J. Townend, G. Booth,
J. Gray (Attendant)
Second Row: E. Mahoney, H. Thompson, C. C. Lempriere (Captain), C. Townend,
W. Johnson, A. Plugge. Front Row: G. E. Barker, W. Feetham, J. Holmes.

The first home match was against Liversedge on 21st September, when a try from Jacketts gave Hull a 3-0 victory. Finishing 8th out of 22 (there was no cup competition), the full season's playing record was played 42, won 23, lost 16, three matches were drawn with 259 points for and 158 against. £2,725 was taken on the gate in the 22 home matches and a profit of £485 was made on the season. A loss of £608 was made on the sale of the club's old property on Holderness Road. A total of 3,260 miles was travelled to matches. Two new stands were erected, the east standing having dressing room accommodation under it.

The opposition failed to score in 14 of the matches and L. Donkin became the Club's first Northern Union County Player when he was selected for Yorkshire v Lancashire. Members of the press expressed a wish for a telegraph box to be erected.

Saturday, 23rd May 1896.
The Hull Times,

HULL FOOTBALL CLUB, LIMITED.

ANNUAL MEETING OF SHAREHOLDERS.

The annual general meeting of the Hull Football Club at the Gladstone Hall last night differed in three material points to its predecessors. It was the first statutory meeting since the club's registration as a limited company, the first annual meeting after a season's trial under the Northern Rugby Union, and the first annual meeting after the departure from the Holderness Road ground to the Boulevard. The interest in the doings of the club was apparent by the large attendance of shareholders. Mr. C. Brewer (president) presided, and the other officials present were Messrs. W. C. Townend (vice-capt.), A. Mennell (A team capt.), H. Hildreth and G. W. Stephenson (hon. secs.), A. Bird (hon. treasurer), F. Bowes, J. H. Dannatt, W. D. Lyon, G. Jacketts, J. W. Porter, F. Harrison, and H. Bell (members of committee). The Hon. Solicitor stated that the number of shares allotted by the directors was 442 at £5, which came to the capital sum of £2,210. It was quite possible that a large number of the 442 shares might have to be cancelled after a month's notice by the directors to individuals to whom the shares had been allotted, through unwillingness or inability to pay. The Chairman, in moving the adoption of the report, said they would all be pleased that the season which had passed had been

C. H. Brewer, President Hull F. C. 1898.

a successful one (applause). This success was most gratifying, following as it had done, the great changes which had taken place during the last 12 months — changes which had been very sweeping, and the result of which had been

A CAUSE OF GREAT ANXIETY

to all who had the club's welfare at heart. During the last 12 months they had changed their governing body, their location, and their constitution, and naturally they all felt anxious as to how these radical changes would affect the position of the club. Well, these anxieties had been removed, for the season which had seen them had been one of the most prosperous in the history of the club (applause). The main factor in this success had without doubt been the improved play of the team (applause). He stood before them twelve months ago, and told them that the material they had was of the very best, and only wanted combination and experience to make it one of the best teams in the country. This opinion has been fully justified. The players had made such progress both in style and effectiveness that they had been credited by capable judges in all parts of the country as being far and away the most improved team in the competition. He took that opportunity of congratulating Mr. Lempriere and the rest of the players on the splendid record they had made (cheers). He was only sorry that Mr. Lempriere found it impossible to again undertake the duties of captain (hear, hear). Respecting their severance from the English and Yorkshire Unions, he did not think anyone regretted it. It was a great wrench to sever an association which had lasted so long, but the step was forced upon them, and was taken in the best interests of the club. The Northern Union would become the ruling football power in the North of England. Its death had been regularly prophesied, but today it was lusty and strong and growing in influence and power, and would be living and thriving when those who prophesied its death had been passed away (applause). It had been alleged against it by some of the Yorkshire Union officials that it had endeavoured to make converts by approaching clubs outside its ranks

IN AN UNDERHAND MANNER.

He knew more of the secret history of what had transpired than they who made the statements, and he could tell them that this was false and that the initiative was taken by clubs who wished to join the Northern Union. Having referred to the advantage which followed the change of ground, the Chairman said the club had never been stronger financially or otherwise, but this should not cause them to slacken their efforts until they had been able to buy and pay for their ground, so that they could hand it down as a legacy to those who had to follow them, a fixed and permanent home (loud applause). Mr. W. C. TOWNSEND seconded the motion. MR. CLOSE said the report was not a gilt-edged one, but it was an improvement on the last. He suggested a rider to the report, thanking Messrs. Lempriere and J. S. Barker for giving their services without receiving payment for broken time. Mr. JACKETTS seconded and Mr. GILLYOTT supported the rider, which the Chairman accepted, and the report in its amended form was adopted. The CHAIRMAN then moved, and Mr. TOWNSEND seconded, the adoption of the expenditure and income account. Mr. CLOSE attacked several items, dealing first with the sum of £362 12s. for entertaining visitors, players, &c. He considered the figure should be reduced in the future. They had spent over £2,000 in carrying on the club and he thought that was rather exorbitant. He also criticised the cost of the tour and payment for broken time, complaining that vouchers were not obtainable. He moved, as an amendment, that the account be referred back for particulars with reference to broken time. Mr. ADAMS seconded the amendment, Mr. GILLYOTT said there were certain items which were bristling with irregularities. He did not think

THAT ACCOUNTS WERE FALSIFIED

but if vouchers had been produced there would have been no comment from the watch-dogs of the club. Councillor Gillett, Mr. Ayre, Mr. Lofthouse, Mr. W. Pool, junr., Mr. Danby, Mr. Hardacker, Mr. F. L. Mawer, and Mr. Nightscales continued the discussion, after which the Chairman and Mr. BIRD tendered explanations. Mr. AYRE moved as a further amendment that the expenditure and income account be adopted, and that the ingoing Board obtain vouchers for all payments in future. Mr. Close withdrew his amendment, and seconded Mr. Ayre's proposal, which was carried. The CHAIRMAN moved the adoption of the balance-sheet, Mr. TOWNSEND seconding. Mr. Close again led the attack on the figures and he was followed by Mr. E. T. Sharp, Mr. Bough, Mr. Gillyott, Mr. W. C. Townsend, Mr. Ayre and the Chairman. The motion was eventually agreed to. Mr. Danby moved and Mr. STONEHOUSE seconded, that in future the 'B' team section be dispensed with. It was only natural that Mr. J. W. PORTER should defend its existence, and he did so successfully, the proposition being lost. It was decided to ask the sanction of the Northern Rugby Union to present each of the hon. secretaries with an honorarium, Mr. Stephenson £30 and Mr. Hilldreth £20. A similar resolution was passed with reference to a testimonial to the treasurer (Mr. Bird) £20 being the amount. It was also resolved to ask the consent of the Union to make the following additional testimonials, £15 each to Messrs. H. Bell, G. Jacketts, and A. Mennell. Votes of thanks were accorded to the players, committee, the press, and the Chairman. The election of fifteen directors resulted as follows:- Messrs. Brewer, Porter, Hilldreth, Bell, Stephenson, Mennell, Lyon, Donkin, Whitehead, Gillyott, Braithwaite, Gillett, Simpson, Pool, and Wilkinson. The six highest non-elected came in the following order:- Jacketts, Bowes, Cubley, Bird, Hakes, and Tindle. The old members of the committee who were not elected were Messrs. Cubley, S. A Holmes, F. Tindle, A. Bird, F. Bowes, J. H. Dannatt, G. Jacketts, and F. Harrison. C. Townend was elected captain of the first team, H. Wiles vice-captain, and J. Holmes captain of the 'A' team.

PLAYER RECRUITMENT

Amongst the local teams who have given of their best, Marlborough ranks perhaps first. From this club came Kilburn, Hewer, Larard, Wiles, Wilkinson, Holmes, Sanderson, Brocklebank, Jacques, Twedell, Rhodes and Gill; Forge contributed well in the persons of Will. and Walt. Mansell, and Holt, Galbraith and Sowery; Athletic furnished Taylor, Smales, Leeming, H. Simpson and Brennan; from St. Mary's came Spavieri, Bearpark, W. Goodison, A. Drewery, Padgett and Art. Shepherd; from Britannia, Timson,

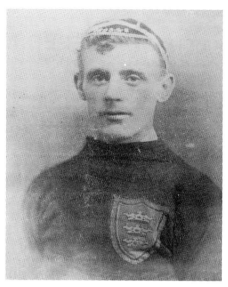

Jack Townend, Vice-Captain 1898
Hull F.C.

Charlie Townend. First made his name with Hull White Star together with his brother Jack, "Cloggy" Fletcher, Charlie Savage and Billy Feetham. Moved to West Hartlepool, returning to captain Hull F.C., a very popular choice.

H. Hildreth, J. S. Barker, A. Plugs, E. Mahoney, L. Donkin, H. Wildes, G. Jacketts, M. Stephenson. T. Wilkinson, C. C. Lempriere, W. Harmer, W. Johnson, H. Thompson, J. Gray, C. Townend, W. Feetham, J. Townend, W. Mansell.

J. Chaffer, G. Booth, whilst Holderness Falcons transferred its whole three-quarter line, consisting of Johnson, Jeffrey and Wright in bulk, supplementing this sacrifice by the release of Harmer. Turning now to the recruiting force within the fold, it may be remarked that ever since the early eighties, the "A" team has been considered absolutely the strongest second string in England. This is a proud boast but it has been substantiated in deeds, not words. Temporarily eclipsed at times, it has always risen superior to misfortune, until today its position is assured. Years ago it went by the name of Wally Roper's Invincibles, and great though its doings in those days, the captaincy of Holmes has inaugurated even a brighter career. A glance at the tabular statement below will give an idea of the strength of the team at various periods:-

	Won	Lost	Drawn	Total
1883-4	24	6	1	31
1885-6	21	3	1	25
1886-7	22	1	1	24
1887-8	20	6	0	26
1889-90	20	5	1	26
1892-3	19	4	2	25
1893-4	24	7	3	34

Brighouse Rangers.

Heckmondwike.

Halifax

Holbeck.

Huddersfield Rugby.

Huddersfield v. Halifax at Huddersfield.

Hunslet.

Leeds.

70

Leeds Parish Church.

Liversedge v. Hunslet at Halifax.

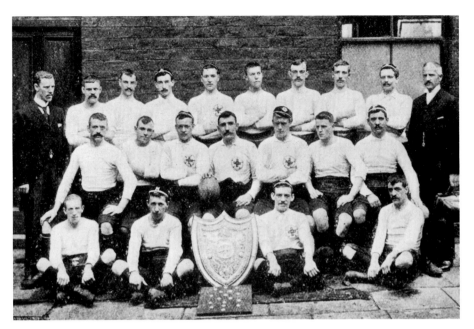

Manningham.

Wakefield Trinity.

Chapter Seven
AND THEN THERE WERE TWO

Hull's fishing industry in the early 1880's was based on Albert Dock with most of the ancillary trades situated in nearby Neptune and English Streets. Two engineering companies, Amos and Smith and C. D. Holmes, had premises in this area and they both supplied steam engines and ships' fittings for the trawler industry for many years.

During the winter of 1882, a group of apprentice boilermakers from both companies met in a house in Vauxhall Grove, off Hessle Road to talk about forming a rugby team. Aged between 15 and 20, this enthusiastic bunch of sportsmen decided on a name — Kingston Amateurs — and agreed on their colours being red jerseys with a broad blue band across the lower chest and sleeves, white trousers and red and white socks. They had to purchase the playing kit themselves. Now they had to find a ground. Their first thoughts were of some waste land in Albert Street (now Gillett Street) off Hessle Road. A distinct advantage was that there was no rent to pay as conditions were very primitive — no stand, no enclosure, a refuse tip at one end and a ditch at the other and one side of the pitch was the raised street flagstones, prompting the ground's nickname 'flag edge touch'. Teams had to change in the nearby hedge bottom and portable goalposts were purchased because the area was used as an itinerants' encampment during the week and permanent goalposts could well have ended up as fire fuel!

A weekly subscription list was set up and fixtures commenced in the Autumn of 1883 and included matches against local teams Falcons, Rifles, St. Mary's, Marlborough, Athletic, Forge, South Myton, Holderness Wanderers 'A', Three Crowns, Melbourne, Southcoates, Sculcoates, St. Georges, South End Rovers, Red Rose and Lockwood Amateurs. The club secretary was Mr. S. J. Ashton of 12 Williams Terrace, Walcott Street and they even fielded an 'A' team some weekends. Players included W. Longthorne, Snowden, Taylor, Miller, Everett, the Milner brothers, Brown, Yates, Green and Ashton.

The next season they moved to a new ground, beyond the railway lines on Anlaby Road and here they paid a rent. Holderness Foundry, White Star, N. E. R. Clerks, Goole, Central Star 'A' and Pottery Rovers appeared on the fixtures list and players included Roe, Carr, Johnson, Purchon and Baker.

Club officials had been elected and rules formed.

Saturday, 1st November 1884.
The Hull and North Lincolnshire Times,

KINGSTON AMATEURS v GOOLE ('A' TEAM). Kingston Amateurs lost. Kingston Amateurs' team:- Hedges, back; White, Bell and Atkinson (captain), three-quarter backs; McKernal and Longthorne, half backs; Hardy, Cater, Rizzey, Hague, Miller, Chapman, Everett, Yeomans and Cavinder, forwards.

Saturday, 29th November 1884.
The Hull and North Lincolnshire Times,

FORGE "A" v KINGSTON AMATEURS. Forge visited the Amateurs, but as the latter wanted to play their own and not the Rugby rules, and not being able to have their own way, left the field, the score then standing — Amateurs, 2 tries (1 disputed) and 1 minor point, to 1 disputed try.

Saturday, 6th December 1884.
The Hull and North Lincolnshire Times,

Kingston Amateurs left their own ground when playing Forge "A". This is exceedingly bad taste. Even under most trying circumstances a club should never leave its own ground, and it is an example which I trust will not be followed by any other of our local teams.

Saturday, 17th January 1885.
The Hull and North Lincolnshire Times,

KINGSTON AMATEURS v ST. MARY'S "A". Played on the Amateurs ground, Hessle Road. Team:- Atkinson, White, Chapman, Hedges, Longthorpe, Cavinder, Milner, Hartly, Cator, Rizzey, Jordan, and Chadwick.

Saturday, 31st January 1885.
The Hull and North Lincolnshire Times,

The hon. sec. of the Kingston Amateurs F.C. writes to say that the game between Kingston Amateurs and South Myton was a first team match (it had been reported as an "A" team game...), and adds, "the game was played to within five minutes of half-time, when one of our men claimed a free kick for off-side play. One of the South Myton men struck at him, and then the home team (South Myton) left the ground."

The club's second Annual Dinner was held in the Albert Hall and Fred Mawer, a Hull member, took the chair at the request of Rovers secretary Mr. Billany.

A third move in three years saw the club playing in Chalk Lane. Now known as Kingston Rovers, the club's secretary was Mr. W. Cavinder of 2 Norway Terrace, Landsdowne Street, Anlaby Road.

Saturday, 19th September 1885.
The Hull and North Lincolnshire Times,

HULL SHAMROCKS v KINGSTON ROVERS. First game as Kingston Rovers. Team:- J. W. Hedges, Atkinson, Milner (captain), J. White, E. Bell, Chapman, Hardy, Milner, Brindle, Jordan, Longthorne, Billany, Cavinder, Rizzey and S. G. Rowe.

Saturday, 26th September 1885,
The Hull and North Lincolnshire Times,

KINGSTON ROVERS v SHAMROCKS. Team:- Hedges, T. Milner, Atkinson, White, Chapman, Bell, Miller, Hardy, Billany, Brindle, Rizzey, Cater, Jordan, Langley, and Yeomans.

Saturday, 16th January 1886.
The Hull and North Lincolnshire Times,

KINGSTON ROVERS FOOTBALL CLUB — The half-yearly meeting of this club was held the other night at the Falcon Inn, Neptune Street. There was a good attendance of members, and Mr. J. Brindle presided. The secretary read the report, which showed the club to be in good condition. The number of matches played up to Saturday, 26th December, by both teams was 20. The first team had played 10 matches and won 10, the total score being 13 goals, 22 tries, and 95 minor points to their opponents 1 goal, 6 tries, and 11 minor points. The 'A' team had played 10 matches, won 7, lost 1, and drawn 2, and scored 6 goals, 18 tries, and 35 minor points to 3 tries and 9 minor points. The secretary will be glad to arrange matches with clubs of the same strength for the following dates:- First team — February 13th, March 20, April 3rd, 10th, and 17th; 'A' team — January 30th, February 20th and 27th, March 13th, 20th, and 27th, April 3rd and 10th.

Saturday, 30th January 1886.
The Hull and North Lincolnshire Times,

KINGSTON ROVERS v WHITE STAR. Kingston Rovers won by 2 tries and 5 minor points to 34 minor points. Team:- A. Atkinson, J. White, T. Milner, R. Chapman, E. Bell, McSherman, Hardy, Cater, Billany, Jordan, Milner, Rowe, Wilson, Hedges, and Baker.

The club entered the *Hull Times* (Newspaper) Cup and were drawn away against Hessle, then an established and successful side led by Len Harrison of Hull. Rovers were so short of funds it was thought the players would have to walk to Hessle to play the cup-tie on Saturday 6th February. But George Whittaker (later to become Club Treasurer) started a subscription list to provide money for the hire of a horse-drawn carriage and while the players travelled in style, it was the club officials who had to walk to the ground! However, it all proved worthwhile as Rovers pulled off a totally unexpected win.

The club had by now acquired quite a formidable playing reputation and Jim White, an expert drop-kicker, was invited to join the senior club, Hull —an offer which was an honour then.

Rovers had a bye in the second round.

On 20th February, 1886, Kingston Rovers beat Three Crowns in the third round of the *Hull Times* Challenge Cup Competition by 1 try and 1 minor point to 9 minor points. Due to the spectators encroaching onto the field of play and interfering with the game, Three Crowns lodged a complaint. It was decided that the match should be played again on a neutral ground. The replay was played on Wednesday 10th March, 1886, on the ground of the Hull Football Club who provided it free of charge.

Three Crowns beat Rovers in the replay but after the match Rovers lodged a complaint against the captain of the Three Crowns team, G. Smelt, who, allegedly, wore boots with protruding spikes during the game. A meeting was held the following evening (March 11th) between representatives from both clubs. The boots in question were produced and it was decided that the boots were of the "usual kind" and did not have any illegal projections.

Bob Atkinson followed Jim White to the Hull club but neither player stayed there for very long, preferring to return to play with Rovers.

Saturday, 1st May 1886.
The Hull and North Lincolnshire Times,

KINGSTON ROVERS FOOTBALL CLUB — The annual meeting of this club was held last night at the Falcon Inn, Neptune Street, when there was a good attendance of members, Mr. W. Roberts presiding. The secretary read the report, which showed the club to be in good condition. The following officers were appointed for the ensuing season:- captain of the first team, T. Milner; vice-captain, W. Longthorne; captain for the second team, W. Roberts; vice-captain, R. Langley; treasurer, S. Mason; hon. secs., L. Billany and E. Bell.

The first team has played 16 matches, won 13, drawn 2, lost 1, Score: 15 goals, 28 tries, and 120 minor points, to their opponents 3 goals, 8 tries, and 30 minor points. Six goals were dropped — J. White (3), T. Milner (2), and J. Hardy (1); five kicked from place — T. Milner (4), and R. Atkinson (1). The other goals were kicked from a rolling ball by T. Milner (3), J. W. White (1). The tries were obtained by R. Chapman (6), J. Hardy (3), T. Brindle (3), G. Rowe (3), W. Longthorne (2), E. Bell (2), W. Cavinder (2), and R. Atkinson, T. Milner, J. W. White, G. Cater, J. Baker, Keith and Markham one each.

The 'A' team has played 11 matches won 7, drawn 3, and lost 1. Score: 6 goals, 18 tries, and 46 minor points, to their opponents 2 goals, 6 tries, and 14 minor points. Five goals were kicked from place by G. Rowe (3), H. McKernan (1), and C. Barker (1), and one dropped by G. Rowe. The tries were obtained by T. Smith (7), G Rowe, H. McKernan (3), W. Roberts (3), and H. Mason, Mawforth, W. Carr, T. Marshal, H. Croft, T. Oliver, and W. Yeomans one each.

New clubs added to the 1886 fixture list included Forge, Central Star, Beverley and Stepney. Bill Keith, a forward, was signed from Trinity and George Batty took up the "umpire's stick" (the forerunner of the touch judge). Rovers entered the new Hull and District Rugby Union Cup and after beating Central Star, Forge and St. Mary's, they lost to Hull 'A' in the final. Press reports of "ill feeling and bitterness between opposing fans" showed that the city of Hull was divided even in those days!

Saturday, 21st August 1886.
The Hull and North Lincolnshire Times,

"HULL TIMES" Challenge Cup 1886-87 competition. In the list of entries for the above mentioned competition, Kingston Rovers are listed as Hull Kingston Rovers.

Saturday, 9th October 1886.
The Hull and North Lincolnshire Times,

A report on the Rugby Union adopting a points system:- A goal scored in any way (dropped, place kicked or from a rolling ball) to count as 3 points and a try 1 point.

Saturday, 30th October 1886.
The Hull and North Lincolnshire Times,

STEPNEY v KINGSTON ROVERS. This match was played on the ground of the former, but, after a pleasant game up to within a few minutes of time, the Rovers left the field on account of a disputed decision. The game ended in a draw.

Saturday, 13th November 1886.
The Hull and North Lincolnshire Times,

A special meeting of the members of the Kingston Rovers Club was held last Saturday at the Falcon Inn, Neptune Street, for the purpose of making a presentation to their treasurer, who is leaving the town. The President, in a well chosen speech, eulogised the character and enumerated the virtues of Mr. Mason, and presented him in the name of the club with a handsome silver guard and scarf-pin, as a token of their regard and esteem, and their appreciation of his efforts to promote the interest of the club. Other members followed the President and wished Mr. Mason every prosperity in his new sphere of labour. The recipient in reply thanked the club for what would be to him a memento of pleasant association. Songs and recitations brought a very enjoyable evening to a close. I need hardly say that I join with the Kingston Rovers in wishing Mr. Mason long life, health, and happiness.

Saturday, 27th November 1886.
The Hull and North Lincolnshire Times,

KINGSTON ROVERS v BEVERLEY. Played on the Rovers ground, Chalk Lane, and resulted in a win for Rovers by 2 tries, 5 minor points, to nil. G. Marshall and G. Cater obtained the tries. W. L. Smithson played an excellent game for Beverley, J. Langley, umpire, G. J. King, referee.

No doubt the announcement that the proceeds of this match would be given towards the funds for the families of the ill-fated sufferers from the Cartago Nova explosion did much to account for the fair field that was present on the Rovers' ground this afternoon. But possibly the certainty of witnessing some good play, when such teams as Rovers (perhaps the best minor team in Hull) and Beverley are pitted against one another. At any rate the gate was a good one, and the spectators were not disappointed with regard to the play. It was somewhat curious coincidence that T. King, who was the donkeyman on board the Cartago Nova, should substitute a gentlemen who failed to turn up as umpire, but so it was.

Rovers: Full back, E. Jarvis; three-quarter backs, T. Miller, G. Marshall, and Atkinson; half backs, J. Stevenson and E. Marshall; forwards, W. Keith (captain), Nelson, Miller, Jordan, Hardy, Cater, Elder, Foster, and Longthorne. Umpire, T. Morley.

Beverley: Full back, T. Rennard, three-quarter backs, Newbold (captain), Brough and Leeming, half backs, A. Jack and W. Smithson; forwards, Watson, A. Newbold, Newmarch, Lundie, Gall, Elwell, Parker, Downs, and Bird. Referee, T. King.

Saturday, 8th January 1887.
The Hull and North Lincolnshire Times,

FORGE v KINGSTON ROVERS. Although Forge beat Kingston Rovers by 1 goal and 4 minor points to 2 minor points (3-0), before commencing the match it was arranged to consider the fixture a draw, and to dispense with tackling — a mere touch to suffice instead.

Kingston Rovers: T. Milner, J. White, G. Roe, R. Atkinson, E. Bell, R. Chapman, W. Keith, J. Elder, J. Stephens, W. Longthorne, G. Cater, A. Jordan, J. Wilson, J. Hardy, R. Milner. Umpire, J. Langley.

NOTE: At this time very few games were being played due to severe frost, this is probably why the game was played as a touch game.

Saturday, 19th February 1887.
The Hull and North Lincolnshire Times,

"HULL TIMES" Challenge Cup, semi-final tie.

KINGSTON ROVERS v YORK 'A'. York 'A' won by 1 try and 2 minor points to 4 minor points (1-0).

Kingston Rovers: R. Atkinson, G. Marshall, T. Milner, W. White, E. Bell, R. Chapman, W. Keith (captain), J. Stephens, J. Hardy, R. Milner, J. Elder, A. Jordan, G. Cater, W. Longthorne, and J. Wilson. Umpire, Mr. Batty.

Saturday, 12th March 1887.
The Hull and North Lincolnshire Times,

Hull and District Rugby Challenge Cup, second round.

FORGE v. KINGSTON ROVERS. Rovers won by 1 try, 3 minor points to 5 minor points (1-0).

Rovers: T. Jarvis, G. Marshall, T. Milner, J. W. White, E. Bell, G. Roe, W. Longthorne, J. Stephens, F. Milner, J. Wilson, E. Elder, T. Foster, G. Cater, J. Hardy, and A. J. Jordan.

Saturday, 19th March 1887.
The Hull and North Lincolnshire Times,

Hull and District Rugby Challenge Cup, third round.

ST. MARY'S v KINGSTON ROVERS. Rovers won by 3 goals, 1 try and 1 minor point to 1 try, 3 minor points (10-1).

Saturday, 2nd April 1887.
The Hull and North Lincolnshire Times,

Hull and District Rugby Challenge Cup, final.

HULL 'A' v KINGSTON ROVERS. Hull 'A' won by 1 goal, 4 minor points to nil (3-0).

Rovers: Atkinson, White, T. Milner, Marshall, E. Bell, Chapman, Keith (captain), Jordan, Stevens, Milner, Wilson, Hardy, Cater, Elder, and Longthorne. Hull 'A' : Bearpark, Shillito, Kilburn, Smith, Hall, Roper (captain), Jacketts, C. Bell, W. Bell, Cockerill, Lowe, Mawer, P. Iveson, Richardson, Stephenson. Umpires, Batty and Whitehead. Referee, Mr. Mortimer of Dewsbury.

Saturday, 9th April 1887.
The Hull and North Lincolnshire Times,

Hull and District Rugby Challenge Cup, after-match dinner.

Both teams were invited by the Rugby Union to dinner at the Salisbury, but whilst the Rovers accepted, the Hull men declined, stating as their reasons (1) that they owed a duty to their own supporters who were waiting to meet them at the Queen's, and (2) that they were anxious for a large amount to be handed over to the charities. As to the first excuse, they certainly owed a duty, not only to the Rugby Union but to their opponents, who, although defeated, were not disgraced; and, as to the second, if the Hull committee were anxious that the charities should have the fullest benefit of the gate, why on earth couldn't they have acted sociably and generously by accepting the invitation and paying for their team's dinner, instead of going to the Queen's? It looked at though they (Hull) meant what they said, when they expressed their sympathy with minor clubs. It's all bosh; they don't care a straw for the younger organisations, and I cannot wonder that the Rovers felt they were slighted.

Opposition from the West Riding of Yorkshire was met for the first time in season 1887/8 and crowds of 2,000 became commonplace at Rovers' new ground at Dairycoates — the Hessle Road Locomotive ground, previously the home of the South Myton Cricket Club, but it proved to be a very wet area.

Only two defeats were suffered during the season. By Hull 'A' in the semi-final of the Rugby Union Cup and by Forge in the Foresters Cup.

Saturday, 3rd September 1887.
The Hull and North Lincolnshire Times,

Kingston Rovers hon. secs., Mr. J. H. Harding and W. Roberts, 9 Arthur's Grove, Manchester Street.

Saturday, 3rd September 1887.
The Hull and North Lincolnshire Times,

KINGSTON ROVERS v SOUTHCOATES 'A'. Rovers opened their new ground on the Hessle Road this afternoon by tackling Southcoates 'A'. They introduced a new feature amongst the minor clubs by playing four three-quarters. About 500 spectators lined the field.

Kingston Rovers: full back, R. Atkinson; three-quarter backs, T. Milner (captain), J. W. White, R. Soulsby, and G. Marshall; half backs, R. Chapman and E. Bell; forwards, W. Longthorne, W. Keith, J. Harding, G. Cater, T. Stephenson, J. Stephenson, J. Wilson, and C. Coyne.

Rovers won by 1 goal, 2 tries, 10 minor points to nil (5-0).

Saturday, 29th October 1887.
The Hull and North Lincolnshire Times,

MELBOURNE v KINGSTON ROVERS (A TEAMS). Melbourne won by 1 try, 3 minor points to 1 minor point (1-0).

Rovers: Mawforth, Toyn, Marshall, C. Baker, T. Smith, Forth, Langley (captain), Harding, Smith, Robinson, Cox, Swan, Neal, Holland, and Stevenson.

Saturday, 5th November 1887.
The Hull and North Lincolnshire Times,

KINGSTON ROVERS v THREE CROWNS. Played on the ground of the former at Dairycoates, Rovers won by 4 goals, 1 try, 5 minor points to nil (13-0).

On Thursday night a large number of the Kingston Rovers club met in the Falcon Inn, Neptune street, to bid farewell to their prominent half back Eli Bell, who left the town yesterday for America. In the course of the evening, which was spent in a jovial manner, Mr. Bell was presented with a silver Albert and medal.

Saturday, 11th February 1888.
The Hull and North Lincolnshire Times,

⁹ HULL TIMES ⁹

FOOTBALL CHALLENGE CUP
COMPETITION

———

The **FINAL ROUND** in connection with the above competition, between

SELBY 'A' AND KINGSTON ROVERS

Will be played (by kind permission of the Hull Football Club) on the

HOLDERNESS ROAD GROUND
THIS DAY, SATURDAY,
FEBRUARY 11TH, 1888,

KICK - OFF AT *3.15* PROMPT,

Admission, 6d. ; Grand Stand and Enclosure, 3d. extra.

Proceeds to be devoted to the **LOCAL MEDICAL CHARITIES,:**

The cup will be handed to the winning team immediately after the match by Mr. F. B. Grotrian, M.P.

The first cup was offered in 1884, and won by Southcoates 'A', who defeated Selby 'A'. The proprietors then offered the present cup under new conditions, to the effect that to become absolute property, it must be won three times altogether or twice in succession by the same club. This cup was first taken by Selby 'A', who defeated the winners of the first trophy.

Onto today's match:- This morning broke in very favourably, and hopes all round were most sanguine. Between twelve and one, however, a change came over the spirit of the dream, for a thunderstorm broke over Hull. Fortunately, we appear to have only received the tail end of the atmospherical ebullition, and after damping the ardour of footballists as well as the ground, the sun appeared on the scene once more accompanied by the bluest of blue skies and the anticipations of the crowds who intended visiting Holderness Road to witness the match brightened proportionately. Everywhere one went the subject of conversation seemed to be embodied in the words "Which team will win?" About two o'clock a large number of persons began to assemble outside the entrance to the excursion platform on the Anlaby Road. Cabs and waggonettes drew up on each side of the road, and the people awaited with patience the arrival of the Selby men and their friends who were coming by a trip due in at 2.19. Like all trips, this one was, of course, late but not so much behind the advertised time as some football trips we have in mind. It was soon seen that quite 800 persons had come from Selby. Many persons said more, but 800 is a moderate estimate. The colours of the club were in nearly every hat, whilst the members of the team were distinguished by each wearing a cherry colour velvet cap with long white tassel. The team drove off to the New Inn, Witham, where they dressed for the conflict. In the neighbourhood of Neptune Street, where the headquarters of Kingston Rovers are situate, the excitement was even more intense. Large numbers of the supporters of the "red and blue" gathered at the headquarters to watch the departure of their pets for the scene of action. Hessle Road was crowded with vehicles ready to convey spectators to the ground and it goes without saying that the Rovers had a large following from this particular district. It was not long after two o'clock when numbers of those interested in the contest began to wend their way along the Holderness Road and in a short space of time a great and continuous flow of people passed through the turnstiles and lined the enclosure on every side. The discussions which took place among the various groups as to the probable result of the match were conducted by the spectators with the utmost good humour, while at the same time the arrival of the combatants was awaited with the most eager expectancy. Until we announce the arrival of the teams it would be interesting to turn our attention to other matters. In the first place, then, the field was covered with a light coating of snow, but, not withstanding this, it was in good condition for play. The wind was not very strong, but what wind there was blew almost directly along the field from the north. In a surprisingly short time the grand and other stands were fully occupied, and the excitement increased to almost fever heat which culminated in a burst of enthusiastic cheering when the Selby men entered, and the applause was still greater when the Kingston Rovers appeared on the scene. The following were the teams:-

Selby 'A': Full back, Smith; three-quarter backs, T. Foster, H. Foster, W. Farley; half-backs, Bell and Wakelin; forwards; J. Palgrave (captain), J. H. Haynes, M. Freeman, H. Firth, J. Jinks, Kelsey, J. Dobson, J. King, and R. Renshaw. Umpire, Mr. Connell.

Kingston Rovers: Back, T. Milner (captain); three-quarter backs, R. Soulsby, G. Marshall, and J. White; half-backs, R. Chapman and G. Cater; forwards, W. Keith, J. Stephens, C. Coyne, W. Longthorne, J. Wilson, J. Hardy, R. Atkinson, T. Stevinson, and G. Rowe. Umpire, Mr. G. Batty. Referee: Mr. E. J. Spink, Wakefield Trinity.

The game, which was a very interesting one, resulted in a win for the Hessle Road men.

THE PRESENTATION OF THE CUP.
SPEECH BY MR. F. B. GROTRIAN, M.P.

Immediately after the conclusion of the game the teams assembled in front of the Grand Stand, where the cup was exhibited prior to presentation by Mr. Grotrian. Silence having been restored.

Mr. F. B. GROTRIAN, M.P. who was received with loud applause, said: "Captain and Men of the Selby Team, Captain Milner and Men of the Kingston Rovers, I have pleasure, Captain Milner, to present to you, as the winner in this contest today, this magnificent challenge cup, which you have well and worthily won. I was not able to be present at the first part of the match, as I had to come from Derby today, where I have been attending to matters in connection with East Hull, but I came down on purpose to present this cup to the winners. I am very glad to have been present to have seen the last half of this match played, and I say it reflects the greatest possible credit upon the winners and upon Hull (cheers). But we must not forget that Selby are entitled also to have a very great deal of credit (applause). It is something to be in the final tie of such a football match as this. That is in itself a great honour. Of course we cannot but be pleased that, Selby having once had the honour of once holding this cup, this time it remains at home, but someday no doubt again Selby will be victorious (applause). I can only say to the Kingston Rovers that to judge by their play which I have seen that however far from home they may roam they will certainly not be far from home when ever it comes to the final tie. In addition to this cup, there will be presented, as a memento also, a silver medal, and a silver medal, also as a memento, to the umpires and to the referee. Now, ladies and gentlemen, it remains only for me to hand over this cup to the winners, and also to ask you, to acknowledge, as we acknowledge, our deep obligation to the Hull Football Club for having so kindly placed this ground at our disposal. It is also a matter of great satisfaction to the donors of this cup that the charities of Hull will benefit by the large gate (cheers). I have now the pleasure to hand over this cup to you —(applause) — and I will ask you to drink the health of the Selby Team" (loud applause).

Captain MILNER: "Here is health to the Selby team".

The other members having drank to the health of their opponents, the captain of the Selby team returned the compliment.

Mr. Grotrian having distributed the medals to the Kingston Rovers' team, and handed one to each of the umpires and the referee.

Captain MILNER called for three cheers for Mr. Grotrian, which were heartily given, and the vast concourse then dispersed.

Saturday, 25th February 1888.
The Hull and North Lincolnshire Times,

FORESTERS CUP COMPETITION

FIRST ROUND.

KINGSTON ROVERS v EAST END. These teams were to meet this afternoon, but East End 'A' did not fulfil their engagement. In spite of a large quantity of snow, Rovers put in an appearance on the field, and, the touch lines having been cleared, Chapman placed the ball and J. Wilson kicked a goal. That was done at half-past three, half an hour after the time when the contest should have commenced — in the presence of the referee, Mr. Antony.

Saturday, 24th March 1888.
The Hull and North Lincolnshire Times,

SEMI FINAL OF THE HULL RUGBY CHALLENGE CUP.

KINGSTON ROVERS v HULL 'A'. Hull 'A' won by 1 goal, 1 try, 2 minors to 8 minors (4-0). Attendance 7,000 to 8,000.

Saturday, 21st April 1888.
The Hull and North Lincolnshire Times,

I hear on very reliable authority that the White Star Football Club, who turned out J. McKie, the Hull three-quarter back, is to be re-formed for next season. They have secured most of their old players, including the two Patersons, Huntsman, Campbell, &c. I learn that they have obtained a field in the neighbourhood of Williamson Street, Holderness Road. W. McMillan, 88 Bright Street, is again the secretary, and will be glad to hear from local clubs as to fixtures.

Saturday, 5th May 1888.
The Hull and North Lincolnshire Times,

KINGSTON ROVERS FOOTBALL CLUB.

ANNUAL DINNER

The annual dinner of the members of the Kingston Rovers Football Club was held on Wednesday in the Lion Hotel, Redbourne Street. There were about eighty gentlemen present, and at the outset of the proceedings they partook of an excellent repast, which was provided by Mr. Jenkinson, on behalf of the host, Mr. Lloyd.

The tablecloth having been removed, Mr. R. T. HUDSON took the chair, and opened the toast list by proposing the toast of "The Queen".

Mr. F. WILSON said he had much pleasure in giving the toast of "Success to the promoters of the *Times* Football Challenge Cup", which the CHAIRMAN remarked, in calling upon the proposer of the sentiment, had been severely fought for before the Kingston Rovers became its custodians.

Mr. GEORGE BATTY supported the proposition, and in doing so said the promoters of the Cup were the first in the field to organise such a thing. Though if they had furthered football to a greater extent, and it was largely owing to the promoters of the *Times* Cup that the Hull Rugby Union had been brought into existence.

The toast was enthusiastically received, and Mr. F. ARTHUR YEO responded, remarking that he could assure them the proprietors would only be too pleased to see Kingston Rovers or any other club win the cup right out. Whenever that was done another cup would be offered the following season (applause). In conclusion, he had one pleasing duty to perform, which was to propose "Long life and continued success to the Kingston Rovers Football Club". The success of the club had been almost phenomenal, and he ventured to think that there were few clubs who could point to a record such as he had seen from a glance at the secretary's report. He hoped next session that the club would go through it without a solitary goal scored against them which stood on record this year. He would couple with the toast the name of Mr. Roberts (applause).

Mr. W. ROBERTS responded to the toast, and remarked that as long as he had belonged to the Kingston Rovers' Club, and he was present when it received its name, he thought the members had worked very well. They had climbed the ladder of success year after year, and he was of opinion that if they continued as they had in the past they would next year win the three cups in the town (hear, hear, and applause).

Mr. M. HARDING read the secretary's report, which showed that the First Team, had played 35 matches, of which they had won 30, lost 2, drawn 3. They had obtained 63 goals, 70 tries, 223 minors; against 1 goal, 9 tries, and 48 minors. The Second Team played 20 matches, and won 12, lost 6, and drew 2. Their score reads:- 14 goals, 22 tries, 87 minors; against 6 goals, 14 tries, 56 minors.

During the evening the First Fifteen were presented with caps, supplied by Mr. F. L. Mawer. Other toasts followed, and in the course of the evening several of those present added to the enjoyment of the proceedings by singing songs, Mr. Harry Fieldhouse was the accompanist.

Doncaster, Heaton and Castleford Hornets were included in the fixture list of 1888/9 when Rovers lost to York 'A' in the semi-final of the *Hull Times* Challenge Cup. A crowd of 6,000 saw the drawn game against Hull 'A' in the Rugby Union Cup at Holderness Road and 3,000 somehow crammed into Rovers' ground for the mid-week replay which Hull 'A' won.

Saturday, 16th February 1889.
The Hull and North Lincolnshire Times,

KINGSTON ROVERS v HULL 'A'. An account of a match where Kingston

Rovers (The Redbreasts) beat Hull 'A', by 1 goal, 3 tries and 5 minors to nil (6-0). This was the first time the Hessle Road men had defeated Hull 'A'.

Hull 'A':- Thompson, McKerman, Gretham, Collins, Lyons (captain), Mennell, Snowball, Hardaker, Spicer, Harrison, Barratt, and Saunders, two short. Umpire, Mr. H. J. Dannatt.

Kingston Rovers:- Downs, White, Milner, R. Chapman (captain), E. Bell, Cater, Coyne, Stevenson, Stevens, Rowe, Chapman, Wilson, R. Atkinson, Foster, Pickering. Umpire, Mr. G. Batty. Referee, Mr. G. Johnson, Castleford.

Saturday, 2nd March 1889.
The Hull and North Lincolnshire Times,

The St. John's Ambulance men are a very good sort, but, the way they skip across the field whenever an accident happens, I am really inclined to think they wait behind the ropes actually hoping that somebody will break his back, or, at all evens, his collar bone, so as to give them something to do. It almost makes one think that the rugby game occasionally becomes rough, which of course, is not the fact. It certainly isn't quite so mild and gentle and milk and watery as the lordly game of tennis — heaven forbid that it ever should be —but it is not a game which requires the constant attendance of an ambulance corps with stretchers and surgical appliances.

Rovers moved to their fifth ground in the season 1889/90. It was behind the Star and Garter pub (now 'Rayners') and had previously been used by the Athletic Club who had disbanded. A stand accommodating 250 and a roped enclosure was a big improvement.

Hull Kingston Rovers. Times Cup Winners 1888/89.
Back: (left to right) J. Elder, T. Kay, J. White, R. Atkinson, T. Longthorne, T. Foster, Eli Bell, J. Hardy, T. Stephenson, G. Batty (President).
Second Row: C. Coyne, R. Soulsby, W. Keith (Captain), T. Miller, Wilf Rose.
Front: Sam Morfitt, A. Matthews, J. Joyce, George King, Jim King.

Sam Morfitt joined the club from Hull 'A'.

Saturday, 21st September 1889.
The Hull and North Lincolnshire Times,

KINGSTON ROVERS v BRITANNIA. The initial fixture of the former's card was concluded this afternoon on the Rovers' new ground, Hessle Road.

Rovers:- T. Milner, G. Marshall, J. White, R. Souslby, E. Bell, W. Rose, W. Keith (captain), Stevens, Stephenson, R. Atkinson, King, F. Chapman, G. Cater, C. Coyne, and Hardy.

Rovers lost by 2 goals, 2 tries, 6 minors to 3 goals, 1 try, 2 minors (8-10).

Saturday, 28th September 1889.
The Hull and North Lincolnshire Times,

Kingston Rovers have taken a wise step by securing a ground with better accommodation, and a little more central than last year's ground and I trust that the takings on this new heath will exceed those taken on the old one. However, a good start was made last Saturday in this line, and if that day's attendance continues an average one throughout the season, I have no reason to doubt that theirs will be the second club in Hull — in that respect at any rate.

Sam Morfitt.
Born in Hull in 1869, he played for Holderness Wanderers, Three Crowns, Southcoates and Hull F.C. before joining Rovers. He went to play for West Hartlepool in 1899 where he played for England against Scotland, Wales and Ireland, although typically the great majority of Rugby Union record books have him down as winning all six caps with West Hartlepool – another example of Union prejudice! Morfitt was a centre, 5ft 4ins and weighing 10st 6lbs. He was also capped by Durham and Yorkshire.

The Yorkshire County Football Club are agitating for the purpose of making it illegal to play rugby football between 1st May and 31st August. Probably a resolution to this effect will be carried at the next meeting of the Rugby Football Union — at least I hope so.

Saturday, 12th October 1889.
The Hull and North Lincolnshire Times,

A very ludicrous incident in the above match (Rovers v Selby 'A') was that which occurred when Soulsby kicked the ball over the rope and hit the ham-sandwich man. It's a mercy it didn't upset the basket, it only just missed it. "Sandwich Tommy" is an enthusiastic supporter of the Redbreasts, but I venture to think his ardour would have been damped had his sandwiches been scattered to the four winds of heaven.

Saturday, 2nd November 1889.
The Hull and North Lincolnshire Times,

A gentleman signing himself "an admirer" writing with regard to next Saturday's match promoted by Kingston Rovers in aid of the Hull Royal Infirmary Debt Fund says:- "I am pleased to see the Rovers set the example to our local clubs. I understand Mr. Mowforth's brass band will make this a bumper by assembling in large numbers on the Hessle Road — late Athletic ground, —and show their appreciation of the Redbreasts' efforts in a good cause".

Saturday, 16th November 1889.
The Hull and North Lincolnshire Times,

In the "Athletic Notes" it points out that Hull 'A' and Kingston Rovers have met seven times. Hull 'A' have won 4, Rovers 2, and 1 has been drawn. Also mentioned is the practice of Rovers having a brass band at their matches.

Quote — "for my own part I'd rather go and see a match between Rovers and Hull 'A', with a band, than go and see a game between Hull and Leeds without one".

Wednesday, 8th January 1890.
Hull Daily Mail,

HULL TIMES CHALLENGE CUP COMPETITION

THE OBJECTION AGAINST KINGSTON ROVERS 'A'

DECISION IN FAVOUR OF WHITE STAR

After being beaten by Rovers 'A' in the above competition, White Star lodged a complaint against Rovers for playing Wilkinson, Banks, Longthorne and Chapman who were not bona fide members of the club. A committee meeting on Tuesday, 7th January 1890, rejected the complaint against Wilkinson, Banks, and Longthorne, but upheld the complaint against Chapman. Consequently Kingston Rovers 'A' were disqualified from the *Hull Times* Challenge Cup Competition.

Tuesday, 14th January 1890.
Hull Daily Mail,

HULL TIMES CHALLENGE CUP COMPETITION

OBJECTION AGAINST KINGSTON ROVERS

MORFITT DISQUALIFIED

After being beaten by Rovers in the above competition, Forge lodged a complaint against Rovers for playing Morfitt who, Forge claimed, was not a bona fide member of the Rovers club. Apparently although Morfitt had played six matches for Rovers prior to the cup game, Forge claimed that these matches had been arranged for the purpose of rendering him eligible. The committee were of the opinion that Rovers had misconstrued the rules and were ordered to re-play the match on a neutral ground, barring Morfitt.

Thursday, 16th January 1890.
Hull Daily Mail,

KINGSTON ROVERS v FORGE. Played on the ground of the Three Crowns Club, Hedon Road, Rovers beat Forge in the re-play of the *Hull Times* Challenge Cup by 3 goals, 4 tries, 11 minors to 1 minor (13-0).

Monday, 10th February 1890.
Hull Daily Mail,

The *Hull Times* Challenge Cup Final.
KINGSTON ROVERS v BRITANNIA. Rovers beat Britannia by 2 tries, 5 minors to 2 minors (2-0).

Thursday, 13th March 1890.
Hull Daily Mail,

A report on the Rovers intention to lodge a complaint after their 2-0 defeat by Hull 'A' on Saturday, 8th March 1890, in the second round of the Hull and District Rugby Union Cup.

HULL AND DISTRICT RUGBY FOOTBALL UNION

Committee meeting last night.

HULL 'A' v KINGSTON ROVERS — on Saturday last Kingston Rovers lodged an objection against the referee that officiated, on grounds that he was not the one that had been appointed by the Rugby Union committee. After carefully considering the matter the committee resolved — "that as the referee was appointed by the secretary of the Union, the committee uphold such appointments, and the objection fee is forfeited".

Monday, 24th March 1890.
Hull Daily Mail,

HULL TIMES CHALLENGE CUP.

Presentation of medals.

An account of the presentation of the above at Kingston Rovers' head-quarters, Abercrombie Hotel, Campbell Street. The final raised £97.11s.4½d at the turnstiles, the most successful since the start of the competition.

A match was played on Good Friday for the first time and the gate money was split 50/50 with opponents Alverthorpe who won by two goals to one. In a season when Foster and Stevenson were outstanding, Rovers played thirty-two games, winning twenty-six, losing four and drawing two. They scored 85 tries, 38 goals and 188 minors against 14 tries, 19 goals and 44 minors. A 'minor' point was awarded to the attacking side when the defending side were forced to

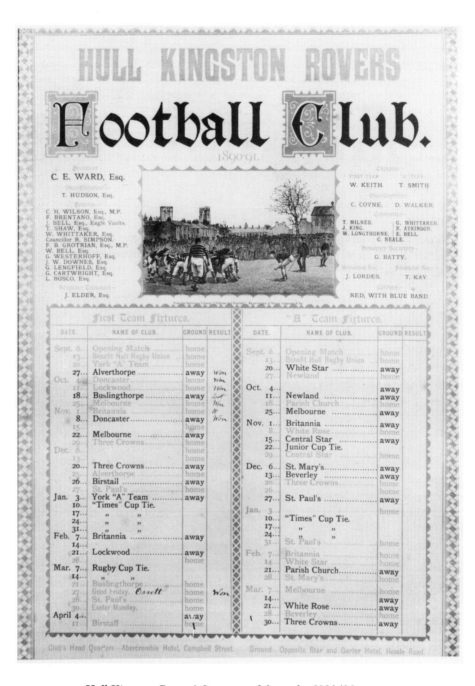

Hull Kingston Rovers' fixture card from the 1890/91 season.

touch down in their own in-goal area. Top scorers Charlie Coyne with 24 tries, skipper Bill Keith (20) while Sam Morfitt placed 8 goals out of 27 attempts plus 2 drop goals. The points scoring system in operation then was: try — 3 points; goal conversion — 2 points; penalty goal —- 3 points; drop goal — 4 points; goal from a mark when player standing still, caught the ball from a kick or a knock-on and then had the option of a free kick at goal or kicking to touch for position — 4 points.

George Batty was still the club's 'umpire' and he was also mine host at the club's headquarters, the Abercrombie Hotel in Campbell Street off Hessle Road. Mr. F. Brentano was Club President.

Fixtures in season 1890/1 included matches against St. Pauls, Alverthorpe, Melbourne, Beverley, Doncaster, Lockwood Arms, Buslingthorpe, Ossett, Outwood Church, Guiseley, Salterhebble, Birstall, Otley, Clarendon and Mytholmroyd, Ony two matches were lost and Rovers became absolute possessors of the *Hull Times* Cup when they won the competition for the third time, beating Britannia in the final thanks to Jim White's trusty left foot.

The first outside talent was introduced into the club with three signings:- Williamson (a half back) and Kilburn (a forward) from Cleckheaton and Jackson from the Pennine area. Sam Morfitt left Rovers for the West Hartlepool club but returned to guest for Rovers during Easter Week.

Tuesday, 7th October 1890.
Hull Daily Mail,

Kingston Rovers, more popularly known as the Robin Redbreasts, achieved a most meritorious victory over the men from the butter-scotch town, known on charts, maps, and other paraphernalia of that kind as Doncaster. Owing to the latter wearing the same old red and blue jerseys as their opponents, the Rovers turned out in county colours of white, and a smart team they looked. Besides this alteration from the usual state of things there was a most amazing point in connection with the game. It commenced with startling punctuality, that is to say it was only half-an-hour late, and our reporter for once in a way had not to fortify himself with his evening meal before he went on duty. Wonderful!

Note: Rovers beat Doncaster by 1 goal, 1 try and 5 minors to nil (4-0).

Tuesday, 18th November 1890.
Hull Daily Mail,

TO THE EDITOR OF THE *HULL DAILY MAIL.*

Sir, As a divergence of opinion seems to exist as to which is the premier club of the town, I, along with many others, think the best way to settle the vexed question would be for Hull to play Kingston Rovers on some Thursday afternoon, the proceeds to be given to the local charities. I feel confident that not only would Rovers play the Hull club a good game, but would beat them with as much ease as did Holbeck on Saturday last; especially if Hull played the same full-back. As there may be (from modesty) a certain amount of diffidence on the part of Rovers in challenging the senior club, I hope the Hull committee will in this case take the initiative. — I am, sir, etc.,

A LOVER OF FOOTBALL.

Tuesday, 25th November 1890.
Hull Daily Mail,

THE HULL AND KINGSTON ROVERS
FOOTBALL CLUB

TO THE EDITOR OF THE *HULL DAILY MAIL*

Sir, I notice in your Saturday's issue of the *Times*, a letter suggesting that the Hull club should play Kingston Rovers for supremacy of the town. Although Hull gave a most wretched exhibition of the game against Holbeck, still it must be admitted that their play in that match was not in their true form, and I think that "a lover of football" must have been dreaming when he thought of such a "suggestion", or must have little knowledge of the game. Then why does he choose the Redbreasts as the team to fight for the position of premier club? Kingston Rovers indeed! I for one fail to see why he should do so, for they have yet to prove that they are the leading minor club, as our friend seems to think them. What about Britannia? I think they have as much right to the title as the Robins. Now, sir, if such a challenge were to be sent out and accepted, and such a match were to be played, my opinion is — without wishing to say anything against the Redbreasts, for I admit they play a good game — that there would be such another miserable fiasco as the one when the Hull team played the 'A' team — in 1887, I think it was, and the year when the 'A' team were invincible — that year Hull was in equally bad form as they are at present. But what was the result? — 6 goals and 1 try to nil, if I remember right. Hoping a "lover of football" will not let such foolish ideas take possession of him again, I will conclude, having, I am afraid, taken up too much of your valuable space already. I am, &c.

AN AMUSED SUPPORTER OF HULL

Hull, 23rd November 1890.

Thursday, 27th November 1890.
Hull Daily Mail,

FOOTBALL : A GOOD SUGGESTION

TO THE EDITOR OF THE HULL *DAILY MAIL*

Sir, I notice in your paper of the 25th an amused supporter of the Hull Football Club giving his opinion respecting "a lover of football's" suggestion, that Kingston Rovers and the Hull 1st team should play a match for the premiership, and the gate to go to charities, which I for one would like to see, as no doubt it would be a large gate, and thereby benefit the charities; but, seeing that the suggestion has not emanated, I take it, from the Kingston Rovers, I think "Lover of Football" will be a long time before he has the pleasure of witnessing such a match, but I do think "An Amused Footballer" must be a very great supporter of the Hull Club and a little biased against the Rovers, or why the remark "Kingston Rovers, indeed?". He likewise states "what about Britannia?". I remember the match played between the Redbreasts and Britannia, and must admit it was the best match I had seen this season, and I have missed one match only. The science that was shown by the two teams would have served as a good lesson to Hull's "premier team", the play was

"combined" and not "individual". The passing was grand, and as some of the reporters stated, was the "finest exhibition" ever witnessed in the town, and described it as the great "Derby Day" in local circles. In conclusion, I would advise "An Amused Supporter" not to rush into print and state what is not fact, for he says when our premier team and the invincible 'A' team met in 1887, they were in as bad form as at the present time. I think the score was not one minor week by week. However, I don't wish to say anything against the first fifteen, but hope they will be more united and gain their good name once more. — Trusting you will find room for this rather lengthy note in your valuable paper yours, &c., BEVERLEY
Hodgson Street, Groves, Hull.

Monday, 1st December 1890.
Hull Daily Mail,

THE HULL AND KINGSTON ROVERS FOOTBALL CLUB

Sir, Kindly allow another supporter (not by any means "amused") of Hull Football Club to offer an opinion. I really think this meeting of Hull 1st team and Kingston Rovers ought to take place, not with a view to contesting the premiership, but simply to find out if we really have got a thoroughly 1st team. There can be no harm done in bringing the two teams together. In fact the meeting must be productive of good if the gate money goes to the medical charities. I will make another suggestion, let a combined team of Britannia and Rovers meet Hull 1st. It would then be easy to know who should be "on" and who should be "off".
I am sir, &c. WILLOW
Hull, November 27.

Monday, 23rd March 1891.
Hull Daily Mail,

HULL AND DISTRICT RUGBY UNION CUP SEMI FINAL TIES

MELBOURNE v KINGSTON ROVERS — these clubs should have played in the semi-final of the Union Cup Competition, but the Rovers scratched to Melbourne.

KINGSTON ROVERS v BUSLINGTHORPE — Kingston Rovers who scratched to Melbourne took on Buslingthorpe beating them 1 goal, 1 try and 4 minors to nil (4-0).

Thursday, 2nd April 1891.
Hull Daily Mail,

The action of Kingston Rovers in scratching to Melbourne is likely to lead to further unpleasantness. There is not the least doubt that the Rovers have earned for themselves anything but a pleasant reputation by their conduct in this matter, and I am informed that the Rugby Union authorities are now on their track, and at a recent meeting passed a resolution requesting the Kingston

Rovers to pay Melbourne the sum of £8.3s.9d.; £5 for the loss of gate and £3.3s.9d, the amount of expenses incurred in making the requisite preparations for the match.

Melbourne's financial affairs are in anything but a satisfactory condition, and everybody sympathises with them in the loss sustained by the match being off. But the question arises, can the Rugby Association compel the Rovers to pay the sum? Kingston Rovers may reply, we can do as we like about scratching; no one can compel us to play if we are not inclined to do so. I believe this will in effect be their answer, and they will decline to part. The matter will then be taken before the Yorkshire Committee, so that we are likely to witness a sensation.

Monday, 27th April 1891.
Hull Daily Mail,

HULL TIMES COMPETITION CUP
FINAL TIE

KINGSTON ROVERS v BRITANNIA. — Kingston Rovers beat Britannia by 1 goal, 1 try and 3 minors to 1 goal and 3 minors (4-3).

Wednesday, 10th June 1891.
Hull Daily Mail,

YORKSHIRE RUGBY FOOTBALL UNION

ANNUAL GENERAL MEETING

THE PROPOSED HULL DISTRICT

The annual general meeting of the Yorkshire Rugby Union was held at the Queen's Hotel, Leeds, the Rev. Frank Marshall (the President) occupying the chair. There was a capital attendance including representatives of most of the clubs affiliated to the Union, and all the members of the County Committee supported the Chairman. — The first business was the consideration of the balance-sheet, which was adopted. — The next business was the election of representatives on the County Committee of the various districts for the coming year, the result being that Mr. G. Hoskins (Hull) was elected for this district. —It was stated that in Hull and Ouse district, owing to the close voting, a recount had been made. — A resolution was submitted in favour of an alteration of the districts represented on the committee, which would provide for the formation of a fresh district to be called the "East Riding District" which would include the following clubs:- Hull, Beverley, Cottingham, Hull Kingston Rovers, Hull Three Crowns, Hull St. Paul's, Hull St. Mary's, Hull White Star, and Britannia. — It was pointed out in course of the discussion that the resolution was incomplete, and did not make any provision for the other clubs which had previously been included in the "HULL and Ouse District". — The motion was lost by a large large majority. — A resolution was proposed to the effect that in future each district should elect its own representatives on the committeee, but it was lost, the voting being — For, 47; against, 48. —Owing to the late hour which had been reached and the fact that a large

94

number of contentious propositions still remained on the agenda paper, it was decided to adjourn for a fortnight.

21 games out of 30 were won in this season (1891/2) when Britannia were the only local side on Rovers' fixture list. The club's 'A' team won the *Hull Times* Cup, beating York 'A' in the final. The first *XV* included matches against Horbury, Windhill, Paddock, Whitwood, Tadcaster, Selby, Cleckheaton, Batley and Bowling Old Lane.

Rovers entered the Yorkshire Cup for the first time and drew Cottingham in the preliminary round but the villagers conceded the match and Rovers then beat Selby in the first round but then went out to Dewsbury. Top scorers during the season were Charlie Coyne (17 tries) and Bill Keith (12) while R. Atkinson, T. Ripton and H. Walker were the main place kickers.

Thursday, 10th September 1891.
Hull Daily Mail,

The International Football Board, at a meeting on Saturday, August 8th, had under their consideration the mode of scoring, and it was decided to adopt the following:- two points for a try, three points for a penalty goal, four points for a dropped goal or a goal kicked from a rolling ball, and five points for a goal kicked from a try. The Rugby Football Union heartily supported the new method, and not withstanding the fact that it has not yet become law, several clubs in Yorkshire have apparently adopted it.

Monday, 21st December 1891.
Hull Daily Mail,

THE *HULL TIMES* CHALLENGE CUP

FINAL TIE

MATCH POSTPONED

All arrangements were made for the final match between Kingston Rovers 'A' and York 'A' to be played on Saturday on the Hull ground, Holderness Road, on behalf of the local charities, but, unfortunately owing to the hard state of the ground consequent on the frost, the match had to be postponed. The York men were accompanied by a large number of their supporters, but it was decided to admit no spectators to the ground until the referee (Mr. Spinks) had decided whether it was advisable to proceed with the game. On the arrival of both teams the captains were consulted, and while the York chief was willing to play, the home captain was of the opinion that the condition of the ground rendered it advisable to postpone the match. Mr. Spinks then, in conjunction with the two captains, carefully examined the ground, and the former concluded that the game could not be contested, and the teams left the field. It was noticeable that the crowd awaiting outside the gate hissed the Rovers' men and applauded the visitors.

Monday, 1st February 1892.
Hull Daily Mail,

KINGSTON ROVERS v SELBY. On the Rovers' new ground, Boulevard, Rovers beat Selby 7-2.
*First mention of the Boulevard.
    Rovers had leased the ground from the Hull Athletic Club.

Monday, 29th February 1892.
Hull Daily Mail,

KINGSTON ROVERS v ALHAMBRA VARIETY ARTISTES. With the highly commendable object of assisting the medical charities of the town, this match was organised by Messrs. Phillips, McNaughton, and Batty. These gentlemen have worked hard to make the affair a success, and it only remained for the public to give their support to achieve this object. A large number of spectators were present, when the following teams entered the field:-
Rovers: Back, Landon, three-quarter-backs, Bearpark, Reynolds, and Soulsby; half backs, McLoughlin and Smith; forwards, Norfolk, Stephens, Hardy, Smales, Shooter, Hall, Carinder, Moore, and Friston.
Artistes: Messrs. Tom and Fred McNaughton, S. G. Stanley, J. W. Mack, White, Young, Cary, Broom, Miller, Heywood, Parker, Manley, Billy Elliot, Wallacini, Friston, Billy Stonehouse, Breaker and Beevers.
    After the unusual preliminaries, which were immensely relished by the onlookers, Miss Florence Smithers kicked off, the ball being charged down. With the first scrimmage came a difficulty; the "Artistes" refused to put down their heads lest they should lose their wigs or hats. After some remarkably loose play "Mad girl" (Tom McNaughton) obtained possession and galloped down the track, in touch, never stopping until she scored a try. Needless to say the point was disallowed. Play still continued in the same humorous style, and eventually the "Mad Girl" scored again, the point this time being allowed. For this offence she was immediately apprehended by Beevers, the policeman. The kick at goal was a failure. "Silly Billy Elliot" was the next to distinguish himself with a drop goal, which also was a failure. Bob Chapman afterwards removed the play, which had been dangerously near the Rovers' goal, to the other end of the field. Here the Redbreasts were awarded a free-kick for off-side, and were lined up by the policeman before the kick was taken. By following up the homesters were enabled to equalise with a try. The kick at goal was again a failure. After several other ludicrous scenes, the comedians again scored a try. Half time was now called, with the professionals leading with 2 tries to 1 goal.
    During the interval the teams were regaled with turnips and carrots, in lieu of lemons. After these had been consumed the teams again lined up. Norfolk kicked-off, the ball going to the "Mad Girl" again who was promptly tackled. The Artistes' "rear guard", who had been giving a comic acrobatic display, were now called upon to defend their line, which they did right well. Bob Chapman obtained the ball and galloped down the field, and in an attempt to stop him "Mad Girl" again distinguished herself by collaring the 50 flag. The same amusing Artiste was soon afterwards alleged to be hurt, and was tenderly removed to the dressing room by several of her fellow players. She soon

returned, however, with her arm and head bandaged and was received with tremendous cheering. Shortly after Bill Stonehouse made the most brilliant run of the day, going at the rate of four miles an hour, right through the Rovers to the line, where he scored a try. Gibson improved with a neat goal. The closing scenes were enlivened by the "Mad Girl" making another sensational run and scoring a try. The match ended with the score standing as follows:- Artistes, 1 goal and 4 tries (13 points) Rovers, 2 goals, 2 tries (14 points).

Thursday, 3rd March 1892.
Hull Daily Mail,

"This will undoubtedly be the funniest football match ever witnessed in Hull". So read the handbills annnouncing the charity match last Saturday. And they were not far wrong in their prophecy either, for the large audience present thoroughly enjoyed the fun, which lasted the whole of the time the Artistes were on the ground. The entrance of the teams was the means of putting everyone in a jovial humour, the costumes being as varied and as comical as one might wish to behold, especially on the football field. Just imagine the following entering the enclose:- "Mad Girl" (Tom McNaughton). "Silly Kid" (Fred McNaughton), "Shopwalker" (J. W. Mack) "Silly Billy" Elliot, Billy Stonehouse as Jack Tar (!), along with a host of niggers, policemen, clowns, mashers, &c., and then you will have some idea of what took place.

Wednesday, 16th March 1892.
Hull Daily Mail,

Kingston Rovers 'A' have refused to play in the final of the *Hull Times* Challenge Cup competition on the day fixed by the donor of the cup, and under the circumstances Britannia were requested to take their place and oppose York 'A'. The Britons realised, without the slightest hesitation, the charitable object of the competition and unanimously agreed to fill the breach. Their kindness deserves the highest praise.

Arrangements are being made to play the final on the Holderness Road ground on Thursday, the 7th April.

I am told that, although the Rovers were requested time after time to play the final on Thursday afternoon, they stubbornly refused. Their ground of objection was that the charities would suffer if the match was played on any other day than a Saturday, and therefore intimated that the only date they would give was April 30th. To a certain extent Rovers are quite right, but half a loaf is better than no bread at all. York would not give up any of their ordinary fixtures having once travelled to Hull, but were willing to play on a Thursday. Surely the Redbreasts could have made a similar sacrifice. But no, they refused to deviate an inch, and the donor of the cup had no other alternative than to disqualify them. This painful step he took simply because, unless the deadlock was removed, the charities would this season receive none of the money which for years past they have been in the habit of deriving benefit from.

Friday, 1st April 1892.
Hull Daily Mail,

HULL TIMES CHARITY CHALLENGE CUP

A VEXED QUESTION SETTLED

GRACEFUL ACT ON THE PART OF BRITANNIA

The arrangements for the final tie of the *Hull Times* Challenge Cup are now completed, and the unfortunate difference arising through the postponement consequent upon the frost, have happily been settled. As is well known, York 'A' and Kingston Rovers 'A' were to meet in the final, but through Rovers being unable to decide to play on a Thursday, the donors ordered that York 'A' should play Britannia who were beaten by Rovers. The Britannia men offered to play for the sake of the charities on Thursday, April 7th. Then Kingston Rovers raised the question as to whether the receival of medals on the part of Britannia would not constitute professionalism. The Yorkshire County Committee were approached for their ruling on the matter. They appointed Mr. Juno, B. Shaw of York and Mr. G. Hoskins, Hull, to consider the question "of presentation of medals to the Hull Britannia team after playing in the final against York 'A'" — so the circular addressed to the parties concerned ran. The meeting was held last evening at the Station Hotel. Mr. J. B. Shaw, with whom was Mr. G. Hoskins, was voted to the chair, Mr. G. Batty (secretary), Mr. Hudson (vice-president), and Mr. Witty represented Kingston Rovers, Mr. J. Avison (treasurer), York, and Mr. J. B. Beckitt (secretary Britannia), Mr. Wm. Corlyon and Mr. P. Mountain attended on behalf of the donors. The whole question as to dates was fully gone into, but as

THE MATTER WAS AMICABLY SETTLED

no good purpose would be served by recapitulation of the same. — The Chairman, after stating — and he was supported by Mr. Hoskins — that the decision would be duly reported to the Yorkshire Committee, suggested the clubs concerned should consult in private and see if any agreeable settlement could not be arrived at. The wise suggestion was adopted, and as a result of the conference Mr. Avison stated the decision arrived at was to the effect that Kingston Rovers' representatives had consented to their 'A' team playing York 'A' on Thursday next. — The Chairman both Mr. Hoskins and myself are very pleased to hear you have arrived at this decision, we are also very pleased to see that Britannia are such good sportsmen as to give way. I contend, by acting in such an honourable way, they are doing their best, not only for the game, but for the charities, and now the other club is willing to take part, as they have given way. Allow me to congratulate them and thank them. — On the motion of Mr. Batty, seconded by Mr. Corlyon, the Chairman was thanked for his services, and proceedings terminated in a happy manner. — It is only fair to add that York 'A' have taken a neutral position and were perfectly willing to meet either club, their sole objective being to assist the charities. With such a happy termination it only remains for suitable weather and a "monster gate" to achieve the object in view.

Thursday, 7th April 1892.
Hull Daily Mail,

HULL TIMES CHALLENGE CUP COMPETITION
FINAL STRUGGLE

KINGSTON ROVERS 'A' v YORK 'A'. Rovers beat York by 1 goal, 1 try and 5 minors to 1 minor (7-0).

Thursday, 21st April 1892.
Hull Daily Mail,

Mr. S. Begs, Turk's Head, Mytongate, one of the patrons of Kingston Rovers F.C., has purchased belts which will harmonise with the jerseys worn by the "Redbreasts" to commemorate their victory in the final of the *Hull Times* Challenge Cup competition. The Robins highly appreciate Sam's generosity.

Rovers signed a lease on the Boulevard for a period of three years starting in season 1892/3. Home wins were gained over Pudsey, Alverthorpe, Kendal, Bingley, West Hartlepool and Hebden Bridge but they lost to Bradford in the first round of the Yorkshire Cup.

George William Lofthouse became the youngest-ever player to turn out for the club at the age of 14. Amos Law, a drop-kicker, joined Rovers from Cleckheaton and Huddersfield and other new signings included R. W. "Ginger" Jackson, Eddy Brinham from Newland F.C. and Jack Gilbson from Britannia.

Rovers finished ninth out of fourteen clubs in season 1893/4 when Sowerby Bridge, Goole, West Riding, Normanton, Keighley, Shipley, Armley, Mirfield, Buttershaw, Alverthorpe, Ossett, Pudsey and Bowling Old Lane made up the Intermediate Competition. A new-style league competition was started up. Ripton, Bell, Winter, Keith and Wilson were selected for the Hull and Ouse *XV* against Northern. Keith scored three times and Ripton kicked a conversion goal in their side's 12-9 victory.

The season was not a success — too many of the stalwarts had grown old together and needed replacing.

Monday, 20th November 1893.
Hull Daily Mail,

THE WEATHER AND FOOTBALL

Owing to the gale which prevailed in and around Hull on Saturday, many of the football engagements had to be postponed or cancelled. In many instances the grounds were found to be in such a condition as to absolutely prevent anything like a match being played.

The Kingston Rovers v Alverthorpe match has been postponed to a future date. The gale during the early morning has done considerable damage to the Athletic ground. The goal-posts at the Anlaby Road end have been blown down, whilst the stand on the western side of the field has been completely wrecked.

Tuesday, 30th January 1894.
Hull Daily Mail,

A HULL PLAYER'S TRANSFER

At a meeting of the Yorkshire Rugby Union last night, Tulloch a Hull player, who early in the season went to Heckmondwike, obtained his transfer to Kingston Rovers.

Monday, 12th February 1894.
Hull Daily Mail,

FOOTBALL

HULL TIMES CHALLENGE CUP (No. 3)

FINAL TIE

KINGSTON ROVERS A v BEVERLEY

Rovers lost by 1 try to nil (3-0).

Saturday, 10th February 1894.
The Hull Times,

HULL TIMES CHALLENGE CUP (No. 3)
KINGSTON ROVERS 'A' v BEVERLEY

KINGSTON ROVERS 'A'

With regards the doings of Kingston Rovers 'A' during the season, we are not in a position to publish them owing to the inability of the secretary to supply us with the necessary information. For an 'A' team they are above average strength, and have played well, not only in the *Times* Cup ties, but in their ordinary engagements.

The Rovers' Captain

Mr. Gibson started his football career about 10 years ago, when he played a season with Paragon Amateurs. Then he went to East End, with whom he played a couple of seasons, and then joined Britannia, remaining with that organisation until the beginning of the season. He cast his lot with Kingston Rovers, and was promptly installed captain. The last two seasons he was with Britannia he was second scorer to the lamented Timson. For Rovers, he has not played many times, and, therefore, has not had the opportunity of showing his scoring power. He was one of the Britannia team when they won the Yorkshire Temperance shield in 1890-91, and also when they carried off the Rugby Union Cup in 1891. He was also in the ranks of the Britons on the two occasions upon which they were in the *Times* final. He is 23 years of age, stands 5 feet 4 inches and weighs 10 stone.

On Saturday, 17th March 1894, Kingston Rovers beat Shipley by 7 points to nil, in the Yorkshire Cup. Before the start of the match the Shipley captain, George Bateson, sent a telegram to the Rugby Union objecting to the condition of the referee, Mr. C. Berry, who seemed to be unwell. The Shipley team wanted to consult a doctor but Rovers declined and wanted to go ahead with the fixture.

Shipley, after the match, alleged that during the game Mr. Berry allowed the Rovers' players to run around the touch judges, thus going into touch, and first allowing a try scored by Shipley then changing his mind and disallowing the touchdown.

At a meeting of the Rugy Union at Leeds on Monday, March 20th, it was decided that the tie should be re-played at Castleford and the proceeds go to the County Committee, after the deduction of the club's expenses.

In the replay on Wednesday, March 21st, Rovers beat Shipley by 14 points to nil.

They beat Hunslet 9-3 at home in the second round but went out 4-8 to the West Riding Club in round three. Rovers finished third in the new third competition in 1894/5 behind Pudsey and West Riding. In the Yorkshire Cup they beat Horsforth and then Mytholmroyd before going out to Hunslet in Round Three.

Chapter Eight
UNCHARTED WATERS

Saturday, 7th September 1895.
The Hull Times,

KINGSTON ROVERS FOOTBALL CLUB.

THE SEASON'S PROSPECTS.

A PROMISING LOOKOUT.

Without a doubt, the present football season is *the* football season, so far as the Kingston Rovers Club is concerned. For a considerable number of years the "Robin Redbreasts", as their most enthusiastic supporters so emphatically term them, have been a West Hull football club. However, owng to obvious causes, they played their last match in West Hull at the close of last season. For reasons known to every football enthusiast in the town, the Rovers were compelled — comparatively speaking — to leave their home. There never was a clearer case of Hobson's choice, they had either to stay in West Hull and die, or "flit" into East Hull and live. And there is not the least question but that they have come into East Hull to live. They have gone to the home of football, the place where the Hull club made the pile, and among the people of East Hull, who set themselves up as an example to the football world at large — among the people who, through thick and thin, stuck right manfully to their team. Although their removal, to the mind of all impartial, was clearly unavoidable, the scheme was received with much opposition, and the "croakes" were loud in prognostication that they could not live outside West Hull. Their removal was the cause of losing from the membership role the names of some few old members of the club who have for many years been connected with the Rovers; ever since, in fact, they began to make a name for themselves. This was a fact greatly to be deplored, inasmuch as the dissentient members were men whom we should have imagined would have absolutely been the last to leave the ship whilst in an unsafe position. If, however, their removal lost them a few friends, it has gained them a considerable number of new ones. In fact, we can venture to predict that instead of the Rovers being the sufferers, owing to the very questionable act of the dissentient members, they have gained considerably by the infusion of the new blood on their committee. Among the men who have

THROWN IN THEIR LOT

with the Rovers may be mentioned the following, who are also on the committee, viz:- Messrs. A. Gemmell, the old Southcoates one-time secretary; G. Thompson, a well-known character in football circles during the old "terrier's" day; Bennett Wilson, the Hull and Southcoates player, and our old friend Mr. Charles H. Savage, who has, in collaboration with Mr. T. Ward, taken over the duties of secretary. They have made a considerable number of

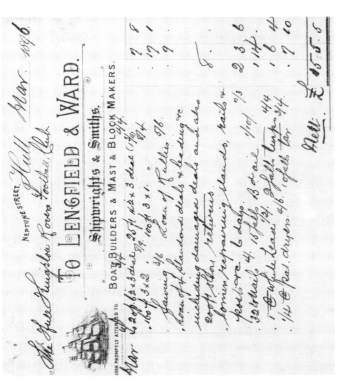

Two accounts relating to repairs to stands at Craven Street.

new members during the last couple of months, including a large number of well-known football enthusiasts. As a matter of fact, during the past two months they have added close upon one hundred names to their membership role. It is well known that their new abode is in Craven Street. At great expense the committee have had their field set in order, and we understand that the nuisance which once existed of large pools of water standing on the ground will now be a thing of the past.

Owing to the formation of

THE NORTHERN LEAGUE

the fixtures with Batley and Wakefield have been scratched, and York and Holbeck taken on in their stead. It is anticipated that fixtures with Dewsbury will also be arranged. Rovers open their season on the 21st with a match against Normanton at Normanton, entertaining Outwood Church the week following. Although not directly connected with the Northern League, the formation of the same has realised the Rovers' committee a certain amount of anxiety, inasmuch as they were in a dilemma as to the effect it would have upon their club. Although the Hull club's new list of fixtures clash upon several occasions with those of the Rovers, this could not, we are led to believe, be avoided, a fact which is sincerely to be regretted, because both clubs will be at a disadvantage. A committee man of the Rovers stated, in conversation the other night, that he considered the formation of the new Northern League was the best thing that could have happened to the Kingston Rovers Club. Also that he now had no doubts as to the promising career before the Rovers.

Hull F. C. were able to offer a higher rent for the Boulevard than Rovers and the Robins moved to their eighth ground in their existence, Craven Street off Holderness Road which had been the home of the old Southcoates Club. Rovers had been promoted to the Second Competition and in their first home game on Saturday 28th, 1895 they beat Outwood Church 29-0. They finished joint second in the league to Shipley and kept a clean sheet in eight of the thirteen home games. Sam Morfitt was now back with the club and he played for England against Scotland, Wales and Ireland and also for Yorkshire against Lancashire, Durham, Oldham, Northumberland, Cumberland, Surrey and Glamorgan. After receiving a bye in the first round of the Yorkshire Cup, they beat Elland at home 12-0, Holbeck at home 15-0 after drawing away 3-3 but they lost in the fourth round at home to Featherstone Rovers 3-6.

Club President, C. E. Ward wrote to the Yorkshire Rugby Union stating that as Rovers were now the only local club in membership of the Rugby Union, they were the senior club and entitled to call themselves the Hull Football Club. The appeal seemed to fall on deaf ears!

Wednesday, 3rd June 1896.
Hull Daily Mail,

KINGSTON ROVERS F.C.

Should the club join the Northern Union?

The annual meeting of the Hull Kingston Rovers Football club was held on

Monday last, at the Plimsoll Hotel, Witham, Mr. C. E. Ward presiding. He said they had been fighting hard to get into the first division of the Yorkshire clubs, and their ambition was likely to be realised if they remained in the Yorkshire Union. If they threw in their lot with the Northern Union they would, at the most, only be included in a second competition. In the Yorkshire Rugby Union there were several good clubs left, notably York, Dewsbury, West Riding, Castleford, and Pudsey; and if they remained true to the old ship, he thought they would certainly be included in the competition with such clubs. He concluded by suggesting they should give the incoming officers and committee power to do what they thought best for the club. There were two sides to the question, and he hoped they would be given an opportunity of

VIEWING THE POSITION COOLLY

and without prejudice (applause). — Mr. W. R. Wilson moved that the matter be left in the hands of the committee. — Mr. C. Coyne said if they stuck to the English Rugby Union and won the Yorkshire Competition they would not meet such good clubs as they would if they went over to the Northern Union. He moved a motion that they settle the matter that night. — Mr. C. Neale seconded Mr. Wilson's motion. — Mr. Mollekin seconded the amendment, and said if they waited any longer they would be too late to get into the Northern Union Yorkshire second section next season, should they decide to go over. — The proposition in favour of the matter being left to the committee to decide was carried by an overwhelming majority. — The meeting then proceeded to elect the officers for next season. Mr. C. E. Ward was unanimously re-elected president, and the vice-presidents were elected as follows: Mr. R. T. Hudson, Mr. Geo. Whittaker, Councillor Simpson, and Mr. S. A. Holmes. Mr. B. R. Wilson was elected hon. treasurer in place of Mr. Neale, who withdrew owing to increased business duties, and the hon. secretaries, Messrs. T. Ward and C. H. Savage, were re-elected. The following constituted the committee:- Messrs. E. Bell, B. R. Wilson, S. Morfitt, Todd, Corry, Coyne, Sellers, Featherstone, and G. Batty. Mr. T. Ripton was re-elected captain, and Mr. H. Tullock (who last season played for Pudsey, but who again has thrown in his lot with the Rovers) was selected vice-captain.

Thursday, 4th June 1896.
Hull Daily Mail,

KINGSTON ROVERS F.C.

TO THE EDITOR OF THE HULL *DAILY MAIL*

Sir, — Seeing the result of the Hull Kingston Rovers F. C. general meeting that I was elected one of the vice-presidents, will you kindly contradict the same as it was done without my knowledge. I have sent to the H.K.R.F.C., asking to withdraw my name. — I am, sir, &c.,
Shalam House, Hull.
                                                                    S. A. HOLMES.

Wednesday, 22nd July 1896.
Hull Daily Mail,

1896-7 FOOTBALL IN HULL

PROPOSED AMALGAMATION OF
RUGBYITES AND ASSOCIATIONISTS

IMPORTANT NEW DEVELOPMENT

It is not unlikely that the football season of 1896-97 will see an important new development in Hull. The lead taken with so much success by many prominent West Riding Rugby Clubs in amalgamating with those attached to the dribbling code has naturally aroused interest in Hull, where the Association game, comparatively new as it is, has attracted marked attention. It is under precisely similar circumstances as are to be found in Hull, or perhaps not so favourable, that amalgamation of this kind has been carried out elsewhere to the infinite satisfaction of the promoters. Then, why should not the same experiment be made in Hull? This question has suggested itself, and, as a result, we understand that negotiations are now in progress for an amalgamation of Kingston Rovers and a new Association Club which has recently been registered under the title of the "Hull Town Association F.C." At present the negotiations are

IN AN EMBRYO STATE

but there seems to be no difficulty in the way of bringing them to a successful issue. If this can be accomplished it will mean that the rugby game will be varied East Hull way by the best exhibition of association the town can give, i.e., when Kingston Rovers are playing away from home, the Craven Street ground will be occupied by the associationists, and vice-versa. Probably another ground will be found for the second eleven teams. This announcement should prove gratifying to patrons of football in East Hull, for there is no reason why both codes should not flourish side by side. We may explain that the new Association club is composed for the most part of the leading players of Hull Albany — a club which did something in the way of making its presence felt last year by entering for the English Amateur and East Riding Cup Competitions. It may reasonably be anticipated that better success will attend their efforts in the future.

Charles Savage, Assistant Secretary of Rovers and later to become the club's first paid secretary, had tremendous vision. He wrote "Association football has been but a minor sport but now I have a notion the interest in it will gradually grow and that it may be at some future time as popular, if not more popular, than is Rugby Football in the district."

The association section, which will run under the name of Hull A.F.C., will provide sport for the public when the Rovers are operating away from home. They commence business next Saturday, when they journey to Bradford to figure in the opening of the new ground there. They have fixtures or promises of fixtures with the following clubs:- Hunslet, Halifax, Leeds, Huddersfield, The Midland Leagues, Doncaster Rovers, and the league (second division) team, Gainsborough Trinity. The last name ought to be a great draw. The "socker" code has come to stay this time. The number of its adherents in Hull has been swelling rapidly of late years, and with a comfortable and convenient ground, and the visit of good elevens, the "gates" should not compare unfavourably by those obtained by the Rugbyites.

To sum up, the prospects of Rovers were never, at any period in their career, brighter than they are at the present time.

Monday, 28th September 1896.
Hull Daily Mail,

INTERNATIONALS FOR ROVERS

It is rumoured that the forward division of Kingston Rovers may be still further strengthened by the inclusion of two new players in the persons of Rhodes and Stark, late of Castleford, both of whom had the honour of donning the jersey for England last season. The matter is still in embryo, and nothing definite is as yet known; but if the men are secured, the Rovers team should not be far out of the running for the championship of the No. 1 competition as well as the Yorkshire Cup.

Rovers moved up to the First Competition in 1896/7 when the West Riding Club dropped out. It was a marvellous season for them — they won the league unbeaten and beat the Rest of the Competition 26-8 in a challenge match and they won the Yorkshire Cup for the first time, beating Shipley in the final 11-5 at Leeds after disposing of Idle, Skipton, Outwood Church, Keighley Shamrocks and Windhill. In the league, Sowerby Bridge refused to travel to

Back Row: F. Pattison, J. Noble, J. Rhodes, A. Kemp, A. Starks, J. Geenty.
Second Row: H. Tullock, R. Rhodes, T. Ripton (Capt.) J. Sparvieri,
M. Gledhill, P. McDermott.
Front Row: D. Morfitt, S. Morfitt, G. Fletcher, C. Coyne.

Hull and Morley conceded the points after the Boxing Day game at Hull had been abandoned and re-arranged for March 29th.

Tuesday, 12th January 1897.
Hull Daily Mail,

KINGSTON ROVERS

ALLEGED PROFESSIONALISM

INQUIRY TO BE HELD

MORFITT, RHODES, STARKS, AND OTHERS

An article detailing the Rugby Union's intentions to summon Hull Kingston Rovers to an inquiry and produce their books, papers, list of players, with the names of the clubs who they last played, and all other necessary information. This was in order to show the "bona fides or otherwise of their players."

RHODES INTERVIEW

In an interview Rhodes denied accepting money for playing with Hull Kingston Rovers, and said that he would rather end his football career than play for a Northern Union team.

Wednesday, 13th January 1897.
Hull Daily Mail,

FOOTBALL PROFESSIONALISM

AWAITING TOMORROW'S INQUIRY

THE SENSATION OF THE FOOTBALL SEASON

The allegations against the Hull Kingston Rovers Football Club was the one subject of conversation yesterday in every district where rugby football has made its presence felt. That the English Rugby Union has ordered an official inquiry in connection with certain players. I am heartily glad, for it will give the Craven Street executive an opportunity of vindicating themselves in the eyes of the public.

The article goes on to accuse, not by name, all the leading amateur rugby clubs in Yorkshire of being steeped in professionalism.

Thursday, 14th January 1897.
Hull Daily Mail,

TONIGHT'S INQUIRY

IS IT FAIR TO ROVERS?

INTEREST IN HULL

This article points out that the onus, so it seems, is on Kingston Rovers to prove their innocence. The article goes on to say that the charges are general and are not very specific, it also asks "who are the accusers?"

Monday, 18th January 1897.
Hull Daily Mail,

RHODES AND CASTLEFORD
IMPORTANT STATEMENT

The following letter has been received from Mr. A. E. Blackburn, the hon. sec., of the Northern Union club, at Castleford:- Sir, — I am requested by my committee to forward you the following facts in reference to the statement by the player J. Rhodes, at the Yorkshire Union meeting on Thursday last.

1st. — "Rhodes has never been offered any inducement whatever, either in cash or promises, to join our club."

2nd. — "On more than one occasion Rhodes has offered to play with our team if we would give him money, which offer has been promptly refused."

3rd. — "Rhodes has stated in the presence of at least half a dozen of our committee that he purposes turning out with our team before the end of the season."

4th. — "When we played Wakefield, Rhodes not only promised to play, but actually told the bagman what size boots he would require. These were obtained specially for him, and taken to Wakefield along with his jersey, &c."

We leave the public to judge the state of this so-called amateur player.

Yours faithfully

A. E. BLACKBURN

hon. sec.

Castleford, 16 January, 1897.

Monday, 25th January 1897.
Hull Daily Mail,

In an article about the Hull Kingston Rovers Football Club, a *Hull Times* reporter interviewed the Rev. Frank Marshall. The Rev. Marshall is described as "An authority concerning all matters relating to amateur football."

It was pointed out to the Rev. Marshall that Jackson (H.K.R.) was not aware that he had become a member of the Northern Union Club Holbeck just by signing their registration forms. The Rev. Marshall replied "so he says; but to my mind the excuse won't hold water. In my eyes, a written application to become a member is precisely the same as signing a registration form. Jackson undoubtedly knew that the Holbeck Club was a Northern Union Club, and by signing their form he went under their banner. Whether he expressed a wish to join is best known to himself."

When asked about Morfitt and the others he said "I would treat them to the same dose and the sooner Yorkshire get rid of quasi-amateurs, the better it will be."

Wednesday, 27th January 1897.
Hull Daily Mail,

Yesterday the *Mail* alluded to the probable attitude of the Northern Union towards players suspended by the English Rugby Union, and I may say that I have this morning received the following letter from a prominent official of the

Robert William Jackson.

Born in 1874, first rugby team he played for was attached to the Commercial School in King Street. After leaving school, he joined Kingston United who played on West Park and then the Newland Club before joining Rovers.
His first match for them was against Selby. He was a keen tackler and a speedy three-quarter.
He was also an accomplished runner, winning the mile race at the Botanic Gardens. Aged 16, he won the eight miles junior championship of Yorkshire at Armley when he was a member of the Spartan Harriers. He was actually suspended by the Athletic Association for a technical offence. He was later beaten over 120 yards by the famous Charlie Harper and in another race by Steve Farrell.
*Jackson also excelled at cricket, playing for Albert United and he won the **Hull Times** bowling prize one year.*

Football Association:- "I have seen in the press, notices to the effect that R. W. Jackson considered the Association game had greater opportunities for him than the rugby code. Until Jackson receives his discharge from suspension by the English Rugby Union, he is not eligible to join any club playing under the English Football Association, as these two bodies recognise each other's suspensions. Neither ought any club to play him whilst under suspension; otherwise they are liable to be dealt with."

Friday, 29th January 1897.
Hull Daily Mail,

KINGSTON ROVERS INQUIRY

PLAYERS AND THE NORTHERN UNION

WHAT MR. HUTCHINSON THINKS

Last night, our Wakefield correspondent had a conversation with Mr. Herbert Hutchinson, secretary of the Yorkshire Senior Competition Committee, as to the attitude the Northern Union would be likely to assume towards Morfitt, Rhodes, Starks, and Jackson, of the Kingston Rovers club, in case they were suspended by the English Union. Mr. Hutchinson said that in the event of the suspension of either Rhodes or Starks by the English Union, they would have to be formally re-instated by the Northern Union before they would be allowed to play, just as Miles of Salford, and others have had to be. Each case would have to be dealt with on its merits, and if it was thought a player had

SUFFERED SUFFICIENT PUNISHMENT

no doubt he would be accepted. But in the case of both Rhodes and Starks he did not think "there was any chance of their getting to play for some time to come." Providing of course they were suspended. "I don't think." Mr. Hutchinson said "Our committee will have them straight away when they have been kicked out of another body. Not likely. We have a dignity to uphold as well as they have, and if they will not come to us in an honourable manner there is no doubt they will find great opportunities when they do want to come." In reply to questions, Mr. Hutchinson admitted that the case of Jackson stood on a different footing. He did not think there would be any opposition to his joining the Northern Union. He had not been suspended for professionalism, but had simply been suspended for signing a Northern Union register — Holbeck to wit.

Monday, 1st February 1897.
Hull Daily Mail,

An article announcing that the second inquiry will be held at the Station Hotel, York, next Tuesday at 2.30 pm.

Wednesday, 3rd February 1897.
Hull Daily Mail,

After a 4½ hour secret inquiry Hull Kingston Rovers were suspended, pending a report by the English Rugby Union Professional Sub-Committee.

Tuesday, 9th February 1897.
Hull Daily Mail,

JACKSON PLAYS ASSOCIATION

HULL TOWN THURSDAY SUSPENDED

R. W. Jackson (H.K.R.) turned out for Hull Town Thursday Association Club. The local Association Committee decided to suspend the club for one month. The club pleaded for leniency, it being their first offence, and the committee modified the penalty to a fortnight.

Friday, 19th February 1897.
Hull Daily Mail,

THE FOOTBALL CRISIS

STARTLING DEVELOPMENT EXPECTED

It is stated in Pudsey today that Pudsey will play Hull Kingston Rovers tomorrow at Hull, even if the professional sub-committee suspend the Rovers. They will be unanimously supported by the three Yorkshire Competitions, who are prepared to declare war if necessary against the Rugby Union, in order to support Hull. Pudsey have selected the strongest team at their disposal.

NOTE: There was no report of this game being played in any of the local papers.

111

Saturday, 20th February 1897.
The Hull Times,

KINGSTON ROVERS

DECISION OF THE PROFESSIONAL SUB-COMMITTEE

At a meeting of the professional sub-committee of the English Rugby Union at York last night, Kingston Rovers were suspended until March 2nd.

Monday, 22nd February 1897.
Hull Daily Mail,

MORFITT'S HOUSE ON FIRE

Some little excitement was caused last night by a report that the Plimsoll Ship Hotel, occupied by S. Morfitt, had caught fire. One of the rooms had become ignited. Assistance was procured, and with the aid of buckets of water, what might have been a serious conflagration was averted. The fire was first noticed by a customer who observed an unusual light in the upstairs room.

Thursday, 4th March 1897.
Hull Daily Mail,

KINGSTON ROVERS v ELLAND

MATCH ABANDONED

Hull Kingston Rovers have sustained another severe disappointment. Every preparation has been made in the hope of entertaining a large crowd on the Craven Street ground this afternoon. But this morning a telegram was received from the Elland secretary stating that it was not possible to raise a team, and suggesting that the match should be played on Monday.

Monday, 29th March 1897.
Hull Daily Mail,

MORLEY SCRATCH

KINGSTON ROVERS TIE WITH FEATHERSTONE

Mr. T. Ward, the secretary of Hull Kingston Rovers, received a communication from the Morley secretary yesterday that his club did not propose to play Rovers this afternoon, and agreeing to give the two points to the Craven Street men. This means the Rovers now tie with Featherstone with 42 points out of a possible 46. They have three matches to play, and have only to gain one point to secure the No. 1 competition trophy. On Thursday Rovers play Pudsey on the Craven Street ground.

Saturday, 17th April 1897.
The Hull and North Lincolnshire Times,

YORKSHIRE CUP.

ROVERS FIGHT FOR IT.

GREAT MEETING AT LEEDS.

DESCRIPTION OF PLAY.
(From our own Reporter)

The present year has, without doubt, been the most eventful one in the whole of the Rovers' career. Their lot has fallen in unpleasant places. They have been buffeted from pillar to post — from Yorkshire to English Union. They have had "double, double, toil and trouble," and yet they have risen, undaunted by the many hard knocks they have received, to demonstrate that talent will force its way to the front in matters football, as well as in matter general. Their triumphs have been as well deserved as they have been hardly earned. There was at the commencement of today's play only one thing that could fill their cup to the brim, and that, of course, was the capture of the old Yorkshire Cup. It was realised that if the unexpected happened, and the Redbreasts failed in the achievement of this — one of their great ambitions — they had still every reason to be proud of their brilliant record, which has brought in its train the trophy of the No. 1 Competition. This is the only true and reliable test of merit, and the Robins, in carrying off the prize, have made good their claim to the title of champions under the banner of the Yorkshire Union. The irony of fate! And this was the club that, at the beginning of the present season, was not considered worthy of a place in the Competition, wherein they have since completely out-distanced all their rivals. Sowerby Bridge, Featherstone, West Riding, all these were preferred, although the Redbreasts had proved their superiority to two out of the three in last year's No. 2 Tournament. Featherstone, the remaining club, was even allowed precedence without the trouble of climbing the ladder. It was only by way of an accident that the path of the Rovers was eventually made smooth. The West Riding Club found themselves unable to carry on the business, and Ripton's brigade stepped in and took their fixtures over bodily.

Their first appearance in the field augured badly for the future, as they were easily beaten. The management lost little time in setting their house in order, and since that day they have carried all before them with the exception of one fixture.

Their difficulties did not end with their struggle to get into "class". Fresh and more serious complications ensued as their success became more pronounced. Jealousy was rampant, and they were requested to appear before the Yorkshire Committee for breaches of the rules relating to professionalism, at the instigation of the parent Union. The allegations were found to be "Not proven", and they breathed freely. It was only for a time, however. The Southerners had been seized with "professional" fever, and meant to blazon forth to the world at large their whole-heartedness in the cause of spotless innocence. An example was needed, and as Rovers were in Yorkshire and the easiest to attack, they were selected. The verdict of the long-suffering Yorkshire Union was reversed and suspension, involving the loss of several Saturday "gates", ensued. This muddled up Rovers' fixtures, a truly stupendous task. These obstacles, in addition to the expenses required to be paid to the English Union, would have been sufficient to discourage the ordinary club, but the Redbreasts, as usual, rose to the occasion and proved superior to them. Surely such enthusiasm and spirit is deserving of a fitting reward.

But by way of consolation they have dropped in for one streak of good fortune. No club could possibly have been more favourably drawn than they in the Cup Ties. They had every round at home till the semi-final stage, which, of course, had to be played on neutral territory. What was more to the point, they were drawn on the weak side, and up to today's match had met nobody that could be considered to be in the same street as themselves.

It is a matter of ancient history that "t'owd tin-pot" once narrowly escaped being brought to the Third Port. That was in the year '84, when the Hull F.C., by successively defeating Gildersome, Leeds St. John's, Heckmondwike, Holbeck and Castleford, reached the final stage, only to be bowled over by Bradford. Since those days attempted tyranny has bred discord, and with the succession of good clubs from the Union, the honour of winning the cup has been shorn of much of its glory. Still the Rovers have done all they have been asked to do in no half-hearted manner.

As a consequence of their meeting inferior teams, their scoring has been prolific, whilst their defence, hardly so good as their attack, has only been penetrated twice. In the first round, they met and vanquished Idle by 20 points to 6, the two tries of the visitors being obtained by the little County sprinter, Frank Murgatroyd, in fine style. In the succeeding round they disposed of Skipton, a club of about the same standing as Idle, by 17 points to nil. The next round saw them walk round the affections of Outwood to the extent of 27 points to nil — a capital result, considering the forward strength of the visitors. The "unknowns", alias the Keighley Shamrocks, were their next guests, and these were sent to the right about by 30 points to nil. History repeated itself last Saturday in the semi-final at York, where they conquered Windhill with identically the same figures. Their passing was something so strange to the Windhillites that they at times became bewildered and stood to look for the ball.

Shipley have had a much greater struggle to reach their present position. In the first round, at Shipley, York made them gallop every inch of the way, but had to eventually retire defeated by 3 tries to nil. Luddendenfoot gave them a tolerably comfortable trip in the following round, but in the third round, although at home, they were once more put on their mettle. Their opponents were Morley, who held the advantage of a goal at half-time. The Shipleyites came again in the second half, and when the whistle blew they had secured a well-earned victory by 12 points to 5. Kinsley, the "dark horse", gave them a fright in the succeeding stage, but were ultimately disposed of by 8 points to 3. Few expected them to vanquish Featherstone in the semi-final last week, but the unexpected happened, though Shipley must be accounted a trifle lucky, as for the major portion of the game they had only 14 men to contend against.

The appended table shows at a glance the comparative results of the contending clubs as far as Cup Ties are concerned:-

ROVERS	Points for	agst	SHIPLEY	Points for	agst
v. Idle	20	6	v. York	9	0
v. Skipton	17	0	v. Luddendenfoot	32	5
v. Outwood Ch'ch	27	0	v. Morley	12	5
v. Keighley Sh'ks	30	0	v. Kinsley	8	3
v. Windhill	30	0	v. Featherstone	4	0
Total	124	6	Total	65	13

As far as previous meetings this season are concerned, Rovers have the better of the argument. At Hull, on November 7th, this season, with a weakened fifteen, they defeated the West Riding contingent by 11 points to nil. On January 2nd, at Shipley, the Redbreasts, after a great fight, emerged victorious by the majority of a single point, their record in all being 16 points as against 4.

Rain had been falling continuously for the whole of the morning, and the consequences were a thoroughly soddened ground and a miserable attendance. Had it not been for the trips from Hull, the ground would have presented an almost deserted appearance. The general opinion was decidedly in favour of Rovers. Sparvieri, who had been on the injured list for the past week, felt himself sufficiently recovered to turn out.

ROVERS TEAM TODAY

INDIVIDUAL SKETCHES

JOE SPARVIERI — FULL BACK

Sparvieri is a Hull lad, born and bred, and made his debut in the football world with the 'B' team of the old St. Mary's F.C., a club which in its time turned out some capital players. His athletic abilities were quickly made manifest, and he received quick promotion into the 'A' and first team. He eventually migrated to the Hull F.C., where he figured in the three-quarter line with success. His record as a goal-kicker while he played with Hull was remarkable, and his figures in this line place him above any local goal-kicker. It is doubtful whether Jim Cheeseborough or Arthur Kilburn in their prime were equal to "Spav", in this particular. Sparvieri ultimately enlisted under the Rovers' banner, first playing three-quarters, and this season full back. As a tackler he is second to none, doesn't know what fear is, and with better judgement would be absolutely unrivalled as a custodian.

SAM MORFIT — THREE QUARTER

The career of Sam Morfitt is almost too well-known to enter into minutely. He has attained the highest honour that it is possible for a footballer to obtain, and this, of itself, is sufficient indication of his great capabilities. He first commenced play with the old Three Crowns, another "nursery" club, but soon found his way into the ranks of the Southcoates F.C., who had their pitch on the Craven Street ground. It will thus be seen that the Rovers' ground is full of tender recollections to "Sammy", and he certainly seems very much at home when performing on it. In those days, he was a diminutive and tricky half back, but when he found his way to West Hartlepool, thanks to a great improvement in his pace, due to nothing else but indomitable perseverance, he was eventually placed in the three-quarter line. Here he proved a great success, and was subsequently included in the Durham County fifteen. The authorities recognised his brilliancy by placing him first reserve in the North and South match, season 94-95, and he luckily fell in the place of Saville. Our representative was present, and had the great satisfaction of witnessing him score the first try of the match. His whole display was so finished and brilliant that the Selection Committee awarded him a permanent place in the English team. His good points as a footballer are numerous.

T. RIPTON — THREE QUARTER (Captain)

No more unassuming and popular player than "Tommy" Ripton exists, and however strong the strictures passed on Rovers, everybody has a good word for the skipper. Ripton is a child of the West, and originally assisted a Hessle Road organisation, known as Parish Church. The Rovers' officials, who are nothing if not enterprising, "discovered" him, and gave him a place in their team. He afterwards assisted Hull, but soon returned to the Rovers' fold, where he has remained ever since. No player has had more to do with the success of his club than the Rovers' captain. For his size he is a wonderful player. His unselfishness is absolutely unrivalled, and Jackson's phenomenal success during the earlier part of the season was in great measure due to this. He is a sure tackler, a deadly "drop" at goal, and can take and give a pass with equal facility. The County authorities in overlooking "Tommy" have done Rovers an extra good turn.

H. TULLOCK — THREE QUARTER

Tullock first sprang to light with the old Newland Club, which included in its ranks R. W. Jackson, Brinham, Wingham, Lax, and other well known sprinters. His latent talents were undoubtedly developed by Herb Bell, who imported him into Britannia, and fed him so persistently that he could scarcely have helped becoming a good back. He eventually shifted quarters to Rovers, where he rendered good service in the three-quarter line. Pudsey had an eye on him, however, and he ultimately threw in his lot with them. They had little reason to regret their "capture", for nobody was more successful than he. This season he returned to his old love, whom he has helped forward to the extent of 4 goals to a dozen tries. His main characteristics are his powerful punting and his strong running, the latter of which would be more effective if he could get his mark sharper, and field the ball better.

D. MORFITT — THREE QUARTER

Daniel is another little fledgeling of Herb Bell's, though, prior to his introduction to Britannia he is said to have played with the 'A' team of West Hartlepool. He is the youngest of the well-known trio of local three-quarters, Jack, Sam, and Dan. He left Britannia to join Rovers, to whom he has remained staunch and true since. He originally played half-back like his brother Sam, and is equally at home as half or three-quarter. Considering his size and weight, he is a good all-round man. He can kick a good length in little room, and is adept at the art of passing.

116

C. COYNE — HALF BACK

Coyne first made his appearance with the old Three Crowns Club, like his confrere, Sam Morfitt. He eventually migrated to Rovers, where he was a continual source of "terror" to his opponents as wing forward. He then sailed under the Hull colours but only for a very short time, and was soon back again with his old "mates". Since the abolition of the obnoxious wing forward he has filled the position of half-back, on and off, with conspicuous success. He is a particularly dangerous man near the line, and if there is a ghost of a chance he will be over. He is more of an offensive than a defensive player, though his penchant for stopping dangerous rushes is well-known. He is an exceedingly "tricky" player, and has the knack of doing the right think at the right moment. His dexterity in grounding the ball is wonderful.

G. M. FLETCHER — HALF BACK

Fletcher sprang originally from the ranks of White Star, a club which included McIntyre, the Townends, and other well-known footballers. He ultimately found his way to the Hull F.C., whom he commenced with in the season '91-92. Following this he fought successively under the banner of Rovers and West Hartlepool. He also migrated to Salford, but only for a brief spell, and he finally settled down with the Redbreasts. It is only lately that he has operated as half back, but he has performed so admirably in this position that there can be no doubt as to its being his proper place. His great and essential characteristics are his extreme coolness and his indomitable pluck. He can be "clashed" fifty times in the course of a match, and his ardour is never damped. He runs strongly and passes with capital judgement. Socially, he is a jolly good fellow, with a dry humour that would be difficult to imitate.

A. STARKS — FORWARD

Starks, who learned his football at Castleford, has, as is well-known, obtained international honours. This is, of itself, a sufficient recommendation for the quality of his play. Probably there is no forward among the Rovers whose style and finish in the open is so much admired. Starks can field the ball remarkably well for a man of such tall stature, and when he does gain possession, his opponents can look to their defence at once. It goes without saying that he is a hard-working forward, and he may invariably be found in the vicinity of the ball. He can kick on occasion, and give and take a pass neatly.

J. RHODES — FORWARD

Rhodes hails from Castleford, and, along with his confrere Starks, threw in his lot with the Robins at the commencement of the present season. He played in all three International matches last season, and would have been almost certain for a place in this year's roll of honour but for a fractured toe, which incapacitated him for some considerable time. He is of Herculean physique, and takes a tremendous lot of stopping when he once gets under way. He is especially dangerous in a line-out, and is essentially a sound and vigorous worker in the pack, where his weight is of very great service. He possesses good judgement.

J. GEENTY — FORWARD

There is an impression abroad that Geenty is an extreme Northerner, but it is an erroneous one, as Geenty is a native of Otley, which, as everybody knows, is

117

in Yorkshire. The greater part of his football career has been passed with the West Hartlepool F.C., which club has, at one time or another, made extensive inroads on our local talent. He gained such a reputation with this club that he speedily found his way into the Durham County team. One trial was sufficient to indicate his merit, and he became a permanent representative. Geenty is an indefatigable worker, both in the pack and in the loose. He follows up quickly, and is a sure tackler. He is noted for his strong bursts, and is almost irresistible if he has a chance near his opponents' lines. Geenty is a good "long" shot at goal.

P. McDERMOTT — FORWARD

McDermott is generally supposed to be a Durhamite, but this is not the case. He is a Tyke, and learned his football with Normanton St. John's, which team he was a member of when they won the Barnsley Hospital Cup. He left Normanton for West Hartlepool, where he was a prominent forward for some time. At the beginning of the present season he, along with his "chum", Geenty, threw in his lot with the Rovers, and proved a decided acquisition. He is a thoroughly conscientious worker from start to finish, and not the least pleasing feature in connection with him is his equanimity.

A. KEMP — FORWARD

Kemp is a Rover, always has been one and probably always will be. Being possessed of a capital physique, he was included in the Rovers' ranks at a very early age. He is very enthusiastic in his club's cause, and nothing has afforded him greater satisfaction than its sudden jump to the front. How he has failed to gain his County cap is a mystery. Certainly he has few superiors in the Broad Acres, and his omission, whilst no doubt beneficial to his club, betrays lack of foresight on the part of the powers that be. However, he has the advantage of youth on his side, and there is ample time for him to receive recognition. His value as a scrimmager is unquestioned, whilst in the loose he is adept at both dribbling and passing. Like Charlie Coyne, he is not a gigantic success as a place-kicker.

M. GLEDHILL — FORWARD

Gledhill hails from Keighley, "where the Shamrocks come from". He played with the 'A' and first teams of Keighley F.C. prior to coming to Hull, when he joined the Redbreasts. He signalised his first appearance with them by scoring a try against Normanton, a point which practically won the match for his side. Probably no player in the Redbreasts' team has improved so much and so quickly as Gledhill. His greatest feat on the

ALBERT KEMP
Captain Kingston Rovers 1898-99.
Born in Hull, he started his rugby career
with the Newbridge club and joined
Rovers in 1894.

118

football field was undoubtedly the wonderful sprint, half the length of the field, against the Shamrocks, which culminated in a well-earned try. He has achieved even greater notoriety as a swimmer than as a footballer, and the training which is required for this branch of sport has no doubt contributed to developing the stamina necessary for football. He is a capital specimen of the healthy Englishman, and is a keen and vigorous player.

J. NOBLE — FORWARD

Noble played with Keighley F.C. previous to joining Rovers, which he did at the commencement of the present season. He is possessed of great powers of endurance, and both takes and gives hard knocks. He is certainly not a "kid-glove" player, but his vigour seldom exceeds the legitimate limits. He is a powerful runner, and can kick a good length. He has been tried as three-quarter back, but he prefers being in the thick of the fight.

R. H. BLADES — FORWARD

"Dick", as he is popularly known to the rest of the team, is an old Keighley player. Along with Noble, he elected to sail under the Rovers' banner at the beginning of the present season. He is of equable disposition, and is scrupulously fair in term "thorough". Whilst he is sharp on the ball, he never shirks his duty in the pack, and can always be relied upon to give a good account of himself.

HEIGHTS, AGES, AND WEIGHTS OF THE PLAYERS

KINGSTON ROVERS.

Back:	Age.	Height.	Weight.	
J. Sparvieri	26	5' 3¾"	11	7
¾ Backs:				
D. Morfitt	24	5' 4"	8	4
S. Morfitt	28	5' 4½"	10	4
T. Ripton	24	5' 5"	9	4½
H. Tullock	21	5' 7"	11	10
½ Backs:				
C. Fletcher	22	5' 8½"	11	10
C. Coyne	24	5' 8½"	11	10
Forwards:				
M. Gledhill	21	5' 9"	14	2
J. Geenty	24	5' 11¾"	13	10
P. McDermott	28	5' 7"	12	4
J. Noble	22	5' 9½"	13	0
R. H. Blades	22	5' 8"	13	0
A. Starks	23	5' 11½"	13	2
J. Rhodes	26	5' 10¾"	14	7
A. Kemp	22	5' 11½"	13	4

Rovers beat Shipley in the Final of the Yorkshire Cup at Leeds by 11-5.

RESULTS 1896-97:-

Date	Club	Ground	Points for	Points agst	Result
Sept. 19	*Featherstone	a	3	9	L
" 26	*Bowling	h	22	3	W
Oct. 3	*Sowerby Bridge	a	12	3	W
" 10	*Cleckheaton	h	14	3	W
" 17	*Elland	a	6	3	W
" 24	*Castleford	h	6	0	W
" 31	*Pudsey	a	0	3	L
Nov. 7	*Shipley	h	11	0	W
" 14	*Featherstone	h	15	5	W
" 21	*Otley	h	20	0	W
" 28	*Wortley	h	13	0	W
Dec. 5	*York	a	11	0	W
" 12	*Dewsbury	a	18	5	W
" 19	*Morley	h	18	0	W
" 25	*Wortley	a	10	3	W
" 26	*Morley	a	8	3	W
" 28	*Featherstone	h	3	0	W
Jan. 2	*Shipley	a	5	4	W
" 9	*Dewsbury	h	8	3	W
" 16	*York	h	11	0	W
Mar. 6	*Cleckheaton	a	13	10	W
" 8	*Elland	h	23	3	W
" 19	*Bowling	h	34	3	W
" 15	Idle (Y.C.T.)	h	20	6	W
" 22	Skipton (Y.C.T.)	h	17	0	W
" 25	*Castleford	a	5	0	W
" 27	Outwood Church (Y.C.T.)	h	27	0	W
April 3	Keighley Shamrocks (Y.C.T.)	h	30	0	W
" 10	Windhill (Semi-final) (Y.C.T.)	York	30	0	W
" 16	Kinsley	h	7	15	L
" 17	Shipley (Final Y.C.T.)	Leeds	11	5	W
" 19	Rest of Competition	h	26	8	W
" 20	*Otley	a	3	5	L

*Denotes competition Matches.

Played 33, Won 29, Lost 4; points for, 472; points against, 99.

Friday, 21st May 1897.
Hull Daily Mail,

KINGSTON ROVERS

NORTHERN UNION MATCHES NEXT SEASON

ONLY CUP COMPETITION

At a meeting of the committee of the Yorkshire Senior Competition last night at Leeds, the secession of the Hull Kingston Rovers Football Club from the English Rugby Union to the Northern Union again came before the meeting, and a deputation from the club, consisting of Mr. Ward (the president) and Mr. Whittaker, waited upon the committee and asked to be allowed to become members of the Northern Union.

After hearing the circumstances, the meeting agreed to recommend Hull Kingston Rovers club to the committee of the Northern Union for membership, which means during the next season that the club will not be concerned in any competition — except the Northern Union cup contest at the end of the season — but will rely upon such ordinary fixtures as can be obtained from the clubs included in the Yorkshire Senior Competition and Lancashire Northern Union organisation.

It will be interesting to see what response the Hull Kingston Rovers' Club will make to the invitation of the Yorkshire Union to send representatives to their meeting on Monday next, especially in view of the fact that the recent deputation to London to meet the committee of the English Rugby Union was to a considerable extent the result of the feeling that the Yorkshire clubs should support the Hull Kingston Rovers, who, it was thought, had been rather hardly dealt with by the authorities in London by their suspension during last season.

It is, however, understood that in taking the present step both the Morley and the Hull Kingston Rovers' clubs have been influenced by the hope that at the end of the next season the committee of the Senior Competition will put in force the rule which says that the lowest club in the competition shall retire and will elect one of them to fill the vacancy.

Tuesday, 25th May 1897.
Hull Daily Mail,

YORKSHIRE CUP

A BRIEF STAY IN HULL

KINGSTON ROVERS RESIGN

A meeting of the committee of the Yorkshire Rugby Union was held last night at Leeds, Mr. A. Hartley (Castleford) presiding, mainly for the purpose of hearing the explanation offered by the two representatives of the Hull Kingston Rovers, who had been asked to attend on the subject of their negotiations with the Northern Rugby Union. No communication had been received in reply to the request, but during the time the meeting was sitting a letter was delivered to the hon. secretary (Mr. J. Miller), and was read by him as follows:

Dear Sir, — I am rather surprised at the tone of your letter, also at the statements which appeared in the papers re the cup. You are reported to have said that no reply had been received by you to the letter sent. I think you must have forgotten that I wrote and informed you that the committee of the above club wished for the Yorkshire Challenge Cup to remain in Hull until the first week in June. As far as the several requests of Mr. G. R. Hill are concerned, I fail to see why we should be in such a great hurry to oblige that gentleman or the English Rugby Union, as they have never done anything to oblige us or Yorkshire in any way, but on the contrary; but I suppose it was returning good for evil. The cup will be returned to you tonight or tomorrow morning, so that there will be plenty of time for it to be on view in London. I also beg to tender you the resignation of Hull Kingston Rovers football club as members of the Yorkshire Rugby Union.
— Yours, &c,   T. WARD, Hon. Sec.

The Chairman: I think they have been very wise to do so. It has saved us the trouble of asking them to do so. I move that it be accepted.

Mr. Avison seconded the resolution; but Mr. Miller, the hon. secretary, proposed as an amendment that the resignation could not be accepted, but that the Hull Kingston Rovers be expelled from the Union.

Mr. Johnson: You can't do that, can you?

The Chairman: It is practically the same thing.

Mr. Johnson: I should second the amendment if it were not for the feeling that, seeing that the resignation has been handed in, we cannot prevent them from resigning.

Mr. Miller: I think we can, seeing that the resignation has only been received just in time. If it had been a few minutes later, I should certainly have moved their expulsion.

Mr. Alderson asked if the Morley club had yet resigned; but no answer was given to the question, and, the resolution being put to the meeting, in the absence of a seconder to the amendment, was carried unanimously.

Mr. Alderson pointed out that the Hull Kingston Rovers must now return the Yorkshire Challenge Cup at once, and Mr. Miller said he had already written asking for it. Under the rules, it must be returned within seven days of the application to join the Northern Union.

At a later stage of the meeting, a letter was read from Mr. C. E. Ward, the president of Hull Kingston Rovers' Club, resigning his position as representative of the Hull and Ouse District on the committee. This was accepted without comment.

Thursday, 17th June 1897.
Hull Daily Mail,

KINGSTON ROVERS

No. 1 COMPETITION THREATEN
LEGAL PROCEEDINGS

The Yorkshire Union No.1 competition met last evening at Leeds, Mr. H. Brown (Morley) presiding.

The committee discussed at length the accounts of the Hull Kingston Rovers (champions) v The Rest of the Competition match at Hull. It appears that Mr. Ward, of the Hull Kingston Rovers, had written, claiming £14.3s.6d. from the competition, including commission at the rate of 15% from the gate money, and expenses of the players, &c. It seems that prior to last year the club on whose ground the championship match was played was entitled to a commission at the rate of 10%. This was abolished, and it was also decided that there should be no free admission of members of the club on whose ground the match was being played. — Mr. Johnson remarked that he noticed that on the occasion of the match at Hull members of the club were being admitted free. It was agreed to take no notice of the account, but to threaten legal proceedings against the club if the competition trophy now held by them is not immediately returned.

Monday, 12th July 1897.
Hull Daily Mail,

In an article about football in Yorkshire it is reported that the Hull Kingston Rovers had still not returned the cup. "If they don't return the cup by Wednesday next a writ will be issued".

Tuesday, 17th August 1897.
Hull Daily Mail,

At a meeting, held at the Queen's Hotel, Charlotte Street, Mr. C. E. Ward, who had been the president of the Hull Kingston Rovers for nine years, decided he had had "a fair innings" and it was time to retire. The vice-president, Mr. Mollekin, was made his successor. Mr. T. Ward vacated the post of secretary and the position was taken by Mr. C. H. Savage.

Sam ("Sammy") Morfitt was proposed as captain. At first he refused, due to him requesting a transfer, but was persuaded to by the members of the club to accept. J. Rhodes was honoured with the post of vice-captain. The president (Mr. Mollekin) announced, to loud applause, that Rhodes and Stark would play for Hull Kingston Rovers again next season.

For the coming season fixtures had been arranged with the following:- Morley, Bradford, Holbeck, Leigh, Walkden, Radcliffe, Hunslet, Eastmoor, Huddersfield, Manningham, and Batley, and that if suitable dates were agreed upon, fixtures could also be arranged with, Leeds Parish Church, Liversedge, Wakefield Trinity, and Ulverstone. There was also a prospect of matches being arranged with Barrow, Stockport, Lancaster, and one or two other leading clubs. The club was also in correspondence with Leeds, Oldham, Castleford, Runcorn, and Hull.

The meeting ended on the decision to form an "A" team.

Thursday, 19th August 1897.
Hull Daily Mail,

NEW FOOTBALL RULE

An article explaining the new rule introduced by the Northern Union. When the ball goes into touch, the ball is to be kicked back into play, replacing the line out. The Northern Union has also changed the scoring to 3 points for a try and 2 points for a goal.

Officials in 1897/8 were Messrs. Ward, Mollekin, Savage, Whittaker, Neale, Foster, Bennett, Hudson, Percy and Wilson.

Rovers were now the only Rugby Union Club in a Northern Union area and an application was made to join the Northern Football Union. However there was no immediate vacancy as Liversedge and Heckmondwike did not amalgamate as expected. The red and whites played friendlies, winning their first game under the new code 31-0 against Crompton. Twenty matches were won, six lost and three drawn. In the Northern Union Cup Rovers beat Marlborough, Morley and Fleetwood but lost to Widnes 5-6 after a 0-0 draw at Craven Street.

Rovers had paid Fleetwood £50 to change their home draw to Hull. W. Guy joined the club — he had played for Tudhoe and Durham. Other signings included Debney and Thorpe from Featherstone, Lindsey and Dugg from Durham, Campsell and Scrupton from Goole and local lads Stephenson and Goodwin from Newton Wanderers and Smith and Draper from Stoneferry.

W. GUY
Vice-Captain Kingston Rovers.
Born in 1874, he started his rugby with Spennymoor Park Rovers and then joined Tudhoe. He captained both these clubs. 5ft 7ins. and 11st. 12lbs. a Durham County half-back, joined Rovers c.1897.

HULL KINGSTON ROVERS F.C.

Dr. to C. E. Ward, 296, Boulevard, Hull, 8.1.1898

Paid to Otley for Guarantee	11	10	0
Advanced to Treasurer for Players (Shipley)	6	0	0
" " " " " (Cleckheaton)	8	0	0
Fares for team to Leeds (Final Yorks Cup)	3	4	9
Paid for labour on field	10	0	0
" to Geenty and McDermott (Suspension)	17	10	0
" Players for Semi-Final Match	7	10	0
" on a/c of Field Rent	4	0	0
" Mr. S. Morfitt on a/c of Club	4	0	0
" for Cinders	2	0	0
" R. W. Jackson during Suspension	10	0	0
" Brown Referee	1	0	0
" Paid Players after Castleford Match 2/- each	2	0	0

Paid Geenty for Club Fares re West Hartlepool	4	0	0
" W. Haller for old Dress Booth	4	10	0
" Blades and Noble after Rest Match	1	0	0
" for Refreshments during training for Cup	2	10	0
" Woodcock on a/c Printing a/c	10	0	0
" Sparrow for Waggonettes	1	18	0
" Wm. Broomfield on a/c Morfitts injury	1	0	0
" Mr. Newton for relaying Ground	37	0	0

TOTAL   £148   12   9

Received on account from treasurer   58   0   0

Total balance due   £ 90   12   9

Saturday, 29th January 1898.
Hull Times,

Rovers have now played nearly every club in the Lancashire Second Division, two in the First, and four in the Yorkshire Senior Class. They have beaten all the first named save Radcliffe, beaten one and lost the other of the seniors, and in their own county have beaten Hunslet and Bradford, drawn Batley, and lost to the last named, Holbeck, and Bradford. Add Morley, defeated by 50 to nil, and a clear indication of the power of the Robins may be had — A deduction which will be useful in view of the coming ties.

Saturday, 5th March 1898.
Hull Times,

The intense hatred and things entertained towards the Hull Club by the average Rovers' partisans may be judged by the fact that on a canard giving the half-time score at the Boulevard as Radcliffe 3 points, Hull nil, being received, a tremendous cheer arose from all around the enclosure. It is to be presumed that now both correct results are known, speculation will be rife as to the possibilities of the local rivals meeting in the semi: and the question naturally arises, who's going to stay at home to look after the bairns, wives, and business?

Tuesday, 21st June 1898.
Hull Daily Mail,

It was reported that at a meeting of the Hull Kingston Rovers at the Neptune Hotel, on Monday, June 20th, the coming season was discussed. Having been excluded from the Senior Competition and due to an alliance of eleven clubs in the First Competition, making it difficult to arrange fixtures, the Hull Kingston Rovers agreed to play in the Second Competition. The decision was made on the understanding that "promotion by merit" was agreed on by the controlling body.

KINGSTON ROVERS' FIXTURES 1898-9

Date		Club	Ground
Sept.	3	*Kinsley	home
"	10	Rochdale Hornets	away
"	17	Morley	home
"	24		away
Oct.	1	*Pontefract	home
"	8	*Goole	away
"	11	(Hull Fair) Bradford	home
"	12	(Hull Fair) Leeds P. Ch.	home
"	15	Widnes	home
"	22	*Normanton	home
"	29	Morley	away
Nov.	5	Rochdale Hornets	home
"		*Rothwell	away
"	19	*York	home
"	26	*Normanton	away
"	3	Wakefield Trinity	home
"	10	Leeds	home
"	17	*Ripon	away
"	24	*Goole	home
"	26	(Bk. Holiday) Widnes	away
"	27	Leeds Parish Church	away
"	31	St. Helen's	home
Jan.	2	Manningham	home
"	7	*York	away
"	14	*Featherstone	home
"	21	*Pontefract	away
"	28	*Outwood Church	away
Feb.	4	*Rothwell	home
"	11	*Kinsley	away
"	14	(Shrove Tue.) *Ripon	home
"	18	*Featherstone	away
"	25	*Outwood Church	home
Mar.	4	Wakefield Trinity	away
"	11	Leeds	away
"	18	N.U.C.T. Manningham	home
"	25	N.U.C.T. ---------	away
"	31	(Good Fri.) Holbeck	home
Apr.	1	Dewsbury	away
"	3	(E. Mon.) Stockport	home
"	4	(E. Tue.) Brighouse R.	home
"	8	Warrington	away
"	15	Dewsbury	home
"	22	Stockport	away
"	29	Cup-tie Final	----

Those matches marked * are in connection with the Second Competition.

Hull Kingston Rovers N.U.F.C. Season 1899-1900. Picture shows:- The team which played in the first "local derby" versus Hull F.C. – at Craven Street on Saturday 16th September 1899. Hull K.R. 1G 2T 8 Pts. Hull 1G 2Pts. (L to R) Back Row: Directors G. Gibbs, J. Mollekin, R. T. Hudson. Standing: J. Debney, Jack Rhodes, Anthony Starks, J. Stephenson, J. Noble, S. Ruddeforth, Director H. Mollekin. Seated: A. Windle, W. Guy, Albert Kemp (capt.) G. Fletcher, R. W. 'Ginger' Jackson. In front: H. Sinclair, T. Ripton, H. Tullock, J. Levett. Scorers: Hull K.R: Goal Tullock (1). Tries: Starks (1), Kemp (1), Hull: Goal W. Jacques (1). Half-time score: H.K.R. 6 pts. Hull nil.

The club was elected into the Second Competition in 1898/9 and won all 17 fixtures, scoring 389 points with only 18 points against. They beat Heckmondwike 21-3 in the challenge match against the bottom team in the Senior Competition and also beat Todmorden 36-0 in the East v West Division Section Winners.

The rules regarding Professionalism were very strict. There was a ceiling of 6/-(30p) per day to recompense players for loss of earnings while playing rugby and players had to be in employment 5½ days a week. Rovers were admitted into full membership of the Yorkshire Northern Union in 1899/1900. In the opening weeks of the season the club was fined £100 and lost two points for playing H. Sinclair without informing the authorities of his change of job and the player himself was suspended until 30th April 1902. The first match was lost 0-3 away at Bradford before the great day. A crowd of 14,000 paid £500 at the first derby match on September 16th, at Craven Street which Rovers won 8-2 with tries from Starks and Kemp and a Tullock goal. The first of many derby matches. The Club Secretary was Chas. H. Savage of 20 Williamson Street and he recorded a club record of 19 successive victories. Rovers finished 6th out of 16 and leading try scorers were Sam Morfitt and H. Tullock. In the Challenge Cup they beat Manningham 11-2 at home but then lost to Broughton Rangers 5-10.

Action fromn Hull K.R. against Wigan at Craven Street.

Rovers playing Halifax at Craven Street.

STATISTICS

HULL F.C. PLAYING RECORD IN
RUGBY UNION COMPETITIONS 1882-1895

	PL	W	D	L	
Yorkshire Cup	29	14	1	14	(Finalists 1884)
Yorkshire Senior Comp	44	11	3	30	

HULL K. R. PLAYING RECORD IN
RUGBY UNION COMPETITIONS 1886-97

	PL	W	D	L	
Hull Times Cup	27	21	3	3	(Winners 1888, 90, 91)
Hull and Dist. R.U. Cup	15	9	2	4	(Finalists 1887)
Hull Foresters Cup	7	4	-	3	(Finalists 1888)
Yorkshire Cup	20	14	1	5	(Winners 1897)
Yorkshire League (various divisions)	102	70	4	28	(Sen. Comp. Winners 1897)

HULL F.C.: PLAYERS' CAREER RECORDS 1882-95
(Competitive matches only)

Player	Seasons	A	G	T
Allen, T.	1892-95	12	-	-
Anderson, J.	1895	3	-	-
Anderson, J. W.	1891	2	-	2
Archer, W.	1894	1	-	-
Barker, G. E.	1895	22	-	1
Bearpark, A. E.	1888-91	7	-	1
Bell, H.	1884-95	30	-	2
Bell, R.	1894	1	-	-
Bell, W.	1885-88	4	1	-
Belt, G. E.	1883-86	12	-	1
Biglin, P.	1895	3	-	-
Bird, A.	1894	11	-	1
Blanchard, R. H.	1887-88	5	-	-
Booth, G.	1895	16	-	-
Boyd, D.	1884	6	3	-
Braithwaite, E. M.	1882-84	2	1	-
Braithwaite, G. W.	1882	1	-	-
Brennan, T. B.	1889-90	3	-	3
Brinham, E.	1894	15	-	-
Bryan, G. E.	1894-95	6	-	1
Calvert, G. E.	1882-90	11	-	3
Calvert, J. F. B.	1882-84	10	4	4
Calvert, W. F. B.	1883-89	19	-	8
Carr, H. R.	1895	2	-	-
Chaffer, J.	1890-95	28	-	2
Close, W. J.	1882	1	-	-
Coates, Rev. C. H.	1886	3	-	-
Cosgrove, T.	1891-92	4	2	1
Coulman, E.	1885-86	4	-	1
Dalling, A. W.	1895	3	-	-
Dickinson, F.	1887	2	-	-
Denton, J.	1894	14	-	-
Donkin, L.	1892-95	29	-	2
Dunkerley, J. A.	1892	2	-	-
Feetham, W.	1894-95	29	-	1
Fletcher, G.	1893-94	3	-	
Galbraith, J. W.	1890-91	4	1	-
Gill, W.	1895	2	-	-
Goften, J. E.	1891	1	-	-
Grant, H.	1892	2	-	-
Harmer, W.	1894-95	25	-	-
Harrison, F.	1890-95	31	-	4

130

Player	Seasons	A	G	T
Harrison, G.	1884-88	15	-	4
Harrison, L.	1886-88	6	-	2
Hewer, T.	1888	3	-	-
Hill, J.	1889-91	5	-	-
Holmes, A. S.	1892-93	3	-	-
Holmes, J.	1894-95	28	-	1
Homan, B.	1895	1	-	-
Hoskins, G. A.	1882-84	4	-	1
Hunter, C.	1894-95	4	-	-
Iveson, A. B.	1884-92	19	1	7
Iveson, A. P.	1884-86	5	-	1
Jacketts, G.	1884-95	56	2	5
Jacques, W.	1894	12	2	-
James, J. R.	1884	5	-	-
Jeffrey, C.	1893-95	23	6	-
Johnson, W.	1893-95	38	2	-
Kay, J.	1886	3	-	-
Kassell, W.	1887	1	2	2
Kennington, G.	1882	1	-	-
Kilburn, A.	1889-90	2	-	-
Knowles, H.	1891	2	-	-
Larard, A.	1893-94	5	-	2
Lee, G. W.	1895	9	-	-
Lempriere, C. C.	1894-95	33	1	3
Lewis, G.	1890	1	-	1
Locking, G.	1894	1	-	-
Lovell, D. R.	1883	2	-	-
Mahoney, E.	1895	1	-	-
Mansell, Walt.	1890-94	8	-	1
Mansell, Will.	1892-95	46	-	4
Marsden, T.	1893-94	19	-	3
Mawer, F.	1883-86	13	-	2
McKay, A.	1892-94	11	-	-
McKay, J.	1894	1	-	-
McLachlan, W.	1890-94	22	-	2
McWatt, W.	1890-91	3	-	-
Mennell, A.	1890	1	-	-
Nightscales, H.	1894	1	-	-
Pattison, F.	1887-90	7	-	-
Read, J. L.	1883	2	-	-
Rhodes, C.	1893-95	12	-	-
Roberts, R.	1893	1	-	-
Robson, H. T.	1895	2	-	-
Roper, W.	1884	2	-	-
Rose, C.	1894	1	-	-

Player	Seasons	A	G	T
Rutter, J.	1889	1	-	-
Savage, C. E.	1894	1	-	-
Shillito, A.	1891-92	4	-	1
Simpson, C.	1884-89	16	-	2
Simpson, H.	1885-90	8	-	1
Smales, C.	1889-94	2	-	-
Smith, G.	1887-88	5	-	4
Smith, H. L.	1882-83	3	-	-
Smith, L. C.	1882	1	-	-
Smithson, A.	1883	2	-	-
Spavieri, J.	1891	2	2	-
Sweeney, F.	1894-95	5	-	-
Tall, W. J.	1882	1	-	-
Teal, W.	1884-91	18	-	4
Thompson, H.	1890-95	27	3	-
Tomlinson, W.	1883-84	4	1	-
Townend, C.	1895	6	-	-
Townend, J.	1894-95	19	-	-
Tuke, M.	1887-90	8	-	1
Tulloch, H.	1893-94	4	-	-
Tweddell, G.	1894-95	6	-	-
Tyacke, A. H.	1882-83	3	-	-
White, J. W.	1886	2	-	-
Whitehead, L.	1882-84	10	-	2
Wiles, H.	1894-95	33	-	3
Wilson, B. R.	1884-86	10	4	-
Wilson, J.	1882-85	11	-	1
Winter, F.	1882-83	4	-	1
Womack, J.	1882	1	-	-
Wray, R.	1894	10	-	-
Wright, D.	1894-95	35	3	4
Wright, W.	1894	2	-	-

HULL KINGSTON ROVERS:
PLAYERS' CAREER RECORDS 1886-97
(Competitive matches only)

Player	Seasons	A	G	T
Allen, O.	1897	2	-	-
Atkinson, R.	1885-95	70	2	8
Banks, W.	1890	1	-	-
Batty, F.	1894	8	-	1
Beharrold	1895	1	-	-
Bell, E.	1886-95	62	1	12
Best	1895	1	-	-
Billany, L.	1886	3	-	-
Blades, R.	1897	28	-	2
Borril, C.	1896	18	14	6
Bray	1894	1	-	-
Brindle, T.	1886	3	-	-
Brinham, E.	1893-96	15	-	-
Brogden	1895	1	-	-
Bulmer, H.	1893	1	-	-
Cater, G.	1886-94	43	-	3
Chapman, F.	1889	3	-	-
Chapman, R.	1886-90	29	2	6
Codd	1895	1	-	-
Cook, J.	1894-97	66	-	9
Cosgrove, T.	1895	3	-	-
Coyne, C.	1888-97	141	-	61
Deeth, W.	1894	1	-	-
Downs, J.	1889-90	6	-	-
Duff, J.	1896	2	-	-
Elder, J.	1887	8	-	-
Elsworthy, E.	1896	22	2	-
Fletcher, G.	1895-97	72	-	12
Foster, H.	1891-96	40	2	4
Foster, T.	1887-90	12	-	1
Friston, T.	1894-95	2	-	-
Frost, T.	1896-97	8	-	-
Garnham	1889	3	-	-
Geenty, J.	1897	31	1	5
Gibson, J.	1894-96	54	2	9
Gledhill, M.	1896-97	55	-	5
Grant	1894	7	-	-
Hardy, J.	1886-91	38	1	1
Hastings	1894	1	-	-
Headon, R.	1897	4	-	-
Hedges, J.	1886	3	-	-

133

Player	Seasons	A	G	T
Holland	1896	1	-	-
Hunter, J.	1894-95	13	1	1
Hunter, R.	1895	11	-	-
Jackson, R. W.	1893-97	26	-	21
Jarvis, T.	1887	2	-	-
Jeffrey, C.	1896	2	-	-
Johnson, J.	1897	3	-	1
Jordan, A.	1886-87	11	-	2
Jordan, D.	1896	5	-	-
Joyce, J.	1890-91	6	5	-
Keith, W.	1887-94	65	2	21
Kemp, A.	1894-97	95	-	12
Kennington, O.	1894-96	74	-	3
Kilbourne, J.	1892-93	3	-	-
King, G.	1890	9	-	-
King, J.	1888-95	23	-	-
Kingston	1894	1	-	-
Langley, J.	1886-88	3	-	-
Langley, R.	1886	1	-	-
Lofthouse, G.	1895-96	31	-	6
Longthorne, W.	1886-89	22	-	-
Lowe, C.	1896	7	-	-
Lund	1895	2	-	-
Marshall, G.	1887-89	24	3	6
Matthews, A.	1891-95	27	-	2
McClaren	1895	2	-	-
McDermott, P.	1897	32	-	4
McIntyre, P.	1896	7	-	-
McSherman	1886	1	-	-
Metcalfe	1897	1	-	-
Milner, R.	1886-88	12	-	2
Milner, T.	1886-92	45	7	-
Moore, W.	1894-96	27	-	3
Morfitt, D.	1895-97	83	13	12
Morfitt, S.	1890-97	47	5	39
Morris	1896	1	-	-
Mowthorpe	1894	1	-	-
Noble, J.	1897	32	-	4
Norfolk, T.	1891-95	12	-	3
Parks, W.	1896	12	-	-
Pattison, F.	1895-97	70	-	3
Pickering, D.	1890-95	31	-	1
Read, J.	1894-95	32	23	5
Rhodes, C.	1894	2	-	-
Rhodes, H.	1888	2	-	-

Player	Seasons	A	G	T
Rhodes, J.	1897	17	-	2
Rhodes, W.	1889	1	-	-
Ripton, T.	1892-97	118	23	20
Rose, W.	1890-96	38	-	8
Rowe, G.	1886-89	22	-	1
Sargeson	1894-95	2	-	-
Scholes	1896	3	-	-
Scholey, R.	1893-94	15	1	-
Simpson, G.	1895-97	57	-	1
Sizer, T.	1895	22	-	1
Smales	1891	1	-	-
Smith, C.	1888	7	-	-
Soulsby, R.	1888-95	48	-	4
Spavieri, J.	1895-97	50	61	9
Starks, A.	1897	23	2	5
Stephens, J.	1887-91	29	-	4
Stephenson, T.	1888-95	64	-	9
Sykes	1897	2	-	-
Tulloch, H.	1894-97	62	6	14
Walker, H.	1891-94	16	-	-
White, J. W.	1886-93	39	7	4
Whittaker, A.	1894-97	50	-	3
Wilson, J.	1886-94	42	9	3
Winter, G.	1890-94	26	-	8
Wray	1895	1	-	-

Notes to appearances and scorers:-

Dates shown are for competitive games only. Some players played over a longer period of time, but not in competition matches. Others played subsequently in Northern Union football. Some also played previously for Kingston Amateurs, White Star and the old Hull F.C.

For conciseness, only the second year of a season is listed. Thus 1888-90 represents seasons 1887-88 to 1889-90 inclusive.

Figures do not include three matches for Rovers where details have not been traced. Scorers are incomplete for two more games. They were also short-handed on a couple of occasions.

Hull and Kingston Rovers each had one obstruction try awarded during the period, which have not been shown in the listing.

BIBLIOGRAPHY

History of Hull and Rovers Football Clubs. C. Townley Fullam 1898.

Hull and Rovers through 88 seasons. Christopher Elton 1981.

Hull Kingston Rovers – A Centenary History. (Lockington Publishing) Michael E. Ulyatt 1983.

Old Faithful – A history of Hull Football Club. (Hutton Press) Michael E. Ulyatt and Bill Dalton 1989.

Hull – A Divided City. Rugby League matches between Hull Kingston Rovers and Hull Football Club 1899-1989. (Hutton Press) Michael E. Ulyatt and Bill Dalton 1990.

The Badminton Magazine of Sports and Pastimes, Vols. I and II. (Longmans Green and Co.) Edited by Alfred E. T. Watson 1895/6.

Rugby League Review March 1948.

The Rugby Football Annual 1889/1900.

Hull Daily Mail; *Yorkshire Post*; *Hull and North Lincolnshire Times* — various issues.

By the same author:

Hull Railway Clerks Cricket Club Centenary, J. S. Sellers and Co. 1973.

Flying Sail, Bradley Publications 1974. Reprinted Mr. Pye Books 1995.

Humber Shipping (with Edward Paget-Tomlinson), Dalesman Books 1979.

Life In Old Hull, Dalesman Books 1983.

Hull Kingston Rovers – A Centenary History, Lockington Publishing 1983.

Trawlermen of Hull, Dalesman Books 1985.

Old Hull Remembered, Dalesman Books 1986.

Barton upon Humber in old picture postcards, European Library 1986.

Old Faithful, Hutton Press 1987.

Hull – A Divided City, Hutton Press 1989.

The Fighting O'Kellys, Hutton Press 1991.

Harold Bowman on Tour Down Under, Hutton Press 1992.

A Brush with Shipping, Richmond and Rigg 1995.

Written as Lesley Bradley:-

Four Hull Tragedies, J. S. Sellers and Co. 1971.